To Tara & Bill,
my prayer is that
the principles in
this book will
help you create an
awesome ministry
team.
God bless you
Bob Pike
Ps. 27:1

BOB PIKE * ROBERT C. FORD * JOHN W. NEWSTROM

THE

FUN

MINUTE

MANAGER

*Create FUNomenal Results Now
Using Fun at Work!*

Creative Training Techniques Press
Eden Prairie, Minnesota

THE FUN MINUTE MANAGER

Copyright 2009 Creative Training Techniques Press

Publisher

Creative Training Techniques Press

14530 Martin Drive

Eden Prairie, MN 55344

ISBN-13: 978-1-935291-04-6

Printed in the USA

www.CreativeTrainingTech.com

To purchase additional copies of this book, or to inquire about bulk discounts and other CTT Press titles, contact us at 866-368-5653 or www.CreativeTrainingTech.com.

Editor: Liz Wheeler

Book designer and illustrator: Alan Pranke *www.amp13.com*

PRAISE FOR THE FUN MINUTE MANAGER

"Successful organizations have a clear vision of where they are headed. They understand what business they are really in. And, most importantly, they develop a culture that supports the vision and business, just as Southwest Airlines did. We hired attitudes that contained a humor and fun component and developed their skills. *The Fun Minute Manager* endorses that concept and gives you a flight plan on how to build a fun, productive and profitable culture."

—Howard Putnam, former CEO of Southwest Airlines, Speaker and Author

"Rare indeed is a book a 'perfect fit' for the time it is birthed. The authors have managed such a glove-to-hand fit with their thoughtful, penetrating, relevant invitation for every manager to fold in fun when work environments so need to find fun."

—Bob Danzig, former CEO of Hearst Newspapers, and Author

"In these tough and difficult times, *The Fun Minute Manager* is a perfect response to build staff morale and effectiveness. Bob Pike is the master of creative solutions that organizations can implement today! He, along with John and Robert, has put that creativity and more into this book. This is a must-read."

—Elliott Masie, Chairman, The Learning CONSORTIUM

"Everybody wants to have fun! You just have to figure out exactly how to develop, expose or invent this. Well, Bob Pike and his cohorts have uncovered the 'keys' to fun and laughter…and productivity, efficiency, creativity, excellence, morale, esprit de corps, and health. The responsibility of incorporating 'fun' into an organization is as important a trait for a CEO to possess as is strategic planning. Having fun is a quality of success. The impact of having fun 'together' is paramount to a family, a neighborhood, a church, a business, and a community. It may seem like a little thing, but it can make a BIG difference."

—C. Kemmons Wilson Jr., Founding Family–Holiday Inns

"*The Fun Minute Manager* is a fun read, and, what's more important, a hands-on, how-to guide to having more fun at work. What can Bob, John, and Robert's lively and helpful new book do for your organization? How about increase morale, creativity, retention and customer satisfaction!"

—Matt Weinstein, Author of *Managing To Have Fun*

"While reading this book, I remembered something Thomas Edison said about work. He said, 'I never did a day's work in my life. It was all fun.' The authors of *The Fun Minute Manager* earnestly remind us that when we lose the fun and joy in our work, we lose our creativity, our inventiveness, our imagination. If every leader in every business follows the authors' simple principles, there's no telling how much ingenuity, creativity, and productivity can be generated. Now, let's go have some fun."

—Paul J. Meyer, *New York Times* best-selling Author and Founder of Success Motivation International, Inc.

"Whatever your style of management, when you couple it with an aspect of fun, your effectiveness increases greatly. As it says on the cover of the cover of my book, *FISH!, Work Made Fun Gets Done. The Fun Minute Manager* shows you how."

—Harry Paul, Co-author of *FiSH! A Remarkable Way to Boost Morale and Improve Results*

"*The Fun Minute Manager* is a great book for anyone that wants his or her organization to be a fun place to work. And who doesn't? In my job as Director of Casting for Walt Disney World (WDW), I knew that if the people we hired weren't having fun, our guests wouldn't either….We did the kinds of things that this book captures so well to make it a fun work environment for our cast members. I would encourage anyone that wants his or her organization's cast members to have more fun at work to read this book. I believe that it is worth your time to both learn and use the concepts and ideas the authors present to make a workplace fun. Both your cast members and the many guests of your organization they touch will thank you for it."

—Duncan Dickson, Director of Casting for Walt Disney World

"*The Fun Minute Manager* will help you transform your workplace from one that is boring, dull, stressful, uncaring, and individual focused to one that is fun, caring, creative, full of laughter, and team focused. What is not to like about this? I can't wait to share this book with my friends."

—Micky Blackwell, former President and COO of Lockheed Martin Aeronautical Systems Sector

"I know Bob Pike. He's a great guy, utterly skillful and fully devoted in his life's Second Half to both success and significance. He and his colleagues make it clear how to braid the two together. Well worth reading."

—Bob Buford, Author of *Halftime* and *Beyond Halftime*

"Bob Pike is the ultimate educator for increasing creativity and having more fun in the workplace. Now, with *The Fun Minute Manager*, Bob, along with his colleagues John Newstrom and Bob Ford, brings you all the insights and tools you need to uplift the spirit of your colleagues, your customers and yourself. Learn what to do, and when and how to do it easily, quickly, and with great fun!"

—Ron Kaufman, Bestselling Author of *UP Your Service!*

"*The Fun Minute Manager* is a practical, cost-effective guide to boosting productivity and making our professional environment more fun for all of our employees. It's a must read!"

—Kelly Nelson, General Manager, Human Resources of AK Steel Corporation

"I've noticed that it is often only the most seriously successful leaders and organizations that take time to create fun in the workplace. In this entertaining and insightful book, the authors reveal secrets to unleashing the power of fun for you and those you work with. I recommend that you drop what you are doing and read *The Fun Minute Manager* …You're sure to benefit a great deal and to have fun in the process."

—Charles C. Manz, prize winning Author of *Emotional Discipline* and *The Leadership Wisdom of Jesus*, and the Nirenberg Professor of Leadership at the University of Massachusetts, Amherst

"Over the many years that I have been actively involved in management, organizational development, and productivity improvement programs, I have observed that highly performing groups of people are usually focused, relaxed, and supportive of one another in getting the job done. *The Fun Minute Manager* is a concise and useful book that is a wonderful resource full of stories, examples, and recommendations that can be used to create both a productive and fun-filled work environment. This book will be a great addition to any manager's toolbox."

—Warren Candy, Senior Vice President (retired) of Allete/Minnesota Power

"If you're not having fun and are not energized by work and the contributions you make, you're simply a mercenary and are selling your soul for shekels. This book paves the way to a truly fun work environment."

—Chris Steele, Vice President (retired) of Financial Shared Services and Accounting Operations, Best Buy, Inc.

"Over the years, research has shown again and again that humor is not only important to relationships and quality of life, but also to productivity. It was nice to have a manager that liked to have fun. What was once optional is now becoming essential as the 20-somethings are now entering the workforce in waves. They have been dubbed 'The Fun Generation.' When they are in jobs where 'fun' is part of the context, their connection with the task at hand increases. *The Fun Minute Manager* will be a valuable tool in the hands of managers who must lead, especially in challenging times."

—Mick Ukleja, Ph.D., Co-author of *Who Are You and What Do You Want? Four Questions That Will Change Your Life*

WE DEDICATE THIS BOOK:

- To our wives, children, and grandchildren, who put countless smiles on our faces
- To the special places where we enjoy spending time—from beach condos in Florida and Hawaii to townhouses in Arizona and rustic cabins in northern Minnesota
- To Frank McLaughlin who played an integral role in our research on fun at work
- To Ken Blanchard who, as Chief Spiritual Officer of the Ken Blanchard Companies, is an iconic Fun Minute Manager
- To those who have strived to inject fun activities into their workplaces and succeeded—even in small ways at first
- To all those persons who have been the brunt of our own attempts at humor and practical jokes and smiled bravely through our efforts at their expense
- To those who encouraged us to believe that organizations should be fun places to work by making them fun for us.
- To God who gave us a sense of humor and Who wants us to have joy.

CONTENTS

CHAPTERS

APPENDICES

FOREWORD

For a long time, I have felt that you should take what you *do* seriously but *yourself* lightly. And I think that is more important today, during tough economic times, than ever before. If you go around taking yourself seriously all the time, you will drive yourself crazy, along with everyone around you. I think we all need to become "Fun Minute Managers."

I have known Bob Pike for a long time and have been an admirer of his ever since we met. He and Robert Ford and John Newstrom have put together a book that belongs in the hands of every leader who has suspected that things would go a little better—especially in the toughest of times—if people would just lighten up a bit and have some fun.

As this book is being published, both the United States and the world at large are in one of the greatest economic crises that any of us can remember. It has been largely brought on, I believe, more by fear than by facts. There are two things that can drive out fear. The first is faith and the belief in a better way of doing things. Bob is chairman of the executive board of a ministry I co-founded called Lead Like Jesus. It is all about challenging people to be servant leaders rather than self-serving leaders, with Jesus as the greatest leadership role model of all time.

Every segment of our world—business, government, education, the professions, nonprofits, and even churches—would all agree that many of the troubles we face today have been caused by self-serving leaders. These leaders think they are the center of the universe and that their needs and desires are most important. No one I talk to today would deny that we are in desperate need of a new leadership role model. I am a firm believer that you finally become an adult when you realize that you are here to give rather than to get, and to serve rather than be served. The most valuable gift we all have to offer is ourselves.

The second thing that will drive out fear, and more to the point of this book, is fun. As you'll learn from Bob, Robert, and John, fun is not synonymous with games. It means a lot of things. It is about ownership and creativity, celebration and recognition. It's about doing the right things in the right way with the right people for the right purpose, and doing more of that each day. It's about letting people find ways to feel pride and have fun with not only the things integral to their jobs and organizations, but also the things they should be celebrating in their lives.

I love a cartoon I saw in another of Bob's books called *Dreams: Working Words of Wit and Wisdom*. It shows a cat dressed in a suit and tie like a businessman, leaning through the door to his office and throwing his hat at the hat rack across the room with a huge grin on his face. The caption reads, "Love what you do, and you'll never work another day in your life." When people are having fun, it is a way of demonstrating that they love what they do. And passion and persistence, coupled with fun, will overcome a multitude of challenges—especially the ones facing us right now.

As the authors well know, my mission in life is to be a loving teacher and example of simple truths. That's exactly what I think you will find in this book—simple truths. For some people, the insights will seem to be counterintuitive. These people have already decided that fun and work don't, can't, and shouldn't mix. They don't want to hear that there is research that supports the idea over and over again that when people are having fun at work, they are more passionate, committed, and devoted to accomplishing results and taking care of people—your customers, your suppliers, people in the community, and each other.

Read *The Fun Minute Manager*. Absorb its teachings, put them into your work life, and make a difference in the lives of everyone you come in contact with. Thanks, Bob, Robert, and John. Here's to all of us becoming "Fun Minute Managers."

Ken Blanchard

—co-author of *The One Minute Manager*® and *The Secret: What Great Leaders Know and Do*

PREFACE

"Are we having fun yet?" is a question often on the lips of employees in too many organizations. If the answer is "no" or "not very often," but you think it should be "yes" for your work group, then this book is for you. Or, if you already believe that having fun at work is desirable but are not sure how to sell it to others at your workplace, *The Fun Minute Manager* will provide a set of useful guidelines to help you overcome their skepticism.

We believe that this book, though short and fun to read, is substantially different from many other books that can also be read within an hour or two. How is this so? First, *The Fun Minute Manager* is based on sound research evidence, not just personal anecdotes or whimsical speculation. Second, it is highly practical, providing useful insights and no-nonsense prescriptions that interested managers can begin applying immediately. Third, it contains a variety of useful appendices. Some of these can be used to generate organization-specific data that will show skeptics that fun at work can improve morale and performance. Our recommendations can also stimulate creative thinking about ways to introduce fun into your workplace. The combination of these multiple ingredients creates a substantive book that will help you chart a course for making your workplace fun. We confidently predict that *The Fun Minute Manager* will remain on your bookshelf for frequent reference for years to come.

The format we have chosen is that of a fictional story. The essence of its message is that fun at work is possible, desirable, and beneficial. We firmly believe that creating a fun work environment can be done easily, quickly, and inexpensively. The key person essential to guiding this process is the Fun Minute Manager—a person who takes personal responsibility for creating a work culture in which fun can flourish, contribute to valued outcomes, and even enhance team performance on several dimensions. By following the journey of discovery that our fun-seeking manager takes in this book, you can change your work environment to one where people actually have fun and enjoy coming to work. This simple, fictionalized story provides an engaging tale in which the Fun Minute Manager:

- discovers why fun is important,
- recognizes that not everyone sees the world through the same mental lens,
- studies the emerging research support for fun work environments,
- involves his or her employees in developing ideas for a fun workplace,
- develops a systematic approach to measuring the benefits of fun,

- anticipates why some employees and some managers might resist having fun at work,

- generates a set of key insights about fun at work, and

- identifies ten key principles for how to make a fun work environment happen.

We recognize that most workplaces are necessarily serious places; they create desired products or provide valued services to their customers and must do so efficiently to survive and prosper in a highly competitive global economy. But we maintain that if these organizations are too serious, they deprive employees of a powerful need for fun, humor, joy, and spontaneity. This deprivation contributes to employee boredom, stress, absenteeism, and turnover, all of which are negative consequences for employers.

Speaking for ourselves, we love a good laugh. We take great joy at seeing smiles on others' faces, especially when employees who truly seem to be having fun at work greet us cheerfully. We wholeheartedly believe that individuals and organizations can benefit from the introduction of fun at work, and that is why we have written this book. Our hope is that you learn how to make your organization a fun place to be. If you do transform yourself into a *Fun Minute Manager*, you are likely to gain the benefits for yourself, your employees, and your organization.

Don't delay; start on your journey of self-discovery to become a *Fun Minute Manager* now, and you will soon reap the rewards of a fun work environment!

A fun work environment is one in which a variety of formal and informal activities regularly occur that are designed to uplift people's spirits and positively and publicly remind people of their value to their managers, their organization, and to each other through the use of humor, playful games, joyful celebrations, opportunities for self-development, or recognition of achievements and milestones.

INTRODUCTION OF TERMS

The emerging literature on fun at work has produced a whole new vocabulary of terms. In this book, you will be introduced to the following concepts:

- Epidemic of Grouchiness
- Fun Epiphany
- Fun Tool Kit
- Fun Work Environment
- Gelotology
- Happiness Quotient
- Smile Barometer
- Smiles per Square Foot
- Surprise Factor
- Terminal Seriousness
- Gospel of Fun

In addition, you'll be exposed to creative job titles such as Corporate Cheerleader, Jollytologist, Funcilitator, Goddess of Fun, Chief Fun Manager, Fun R Us Team Leader, Joy Team Captain, Glee Club Leader, Minister of Fun, No. 1 Funologist, Director of Fun, and Funmeister. Watch closely for these!

INSIGHT ONE

All Work and No Play Makes...

Can you have fun and work at the same time?

"The most wasted of all days is one without laughter."
                                        —*e.e. cummings*
"Time flies when you're having fun."
                                        —*Anonymous*
"Humor promotes creative thinking, mental flexibility, the ability to cope with change...it helps us get along with each other."
                                        —*John Morreall*

"Are we having fun yet?"

Bob Workman, division manager at Apex Environmental Engineering Company, had heard that question many times before, but until now it was always on a TV game show, in a newspaper cartoon, or when he was on the golf course with friends and someone had hit a really bad shot. This time, the question, which was asked in a very sarcastic manner by one of his most respected employees, hit him right between the eyes. Taking the question seriously, Bob stammered, "Uh...uh...I hope so. No, I mean, I guess so. I mean, I'm pretty sure we are. But why do you ask?"

"Because I'm sure the heck not!" the engineer retorted as he spun on his heel and marched stiffly down the hallway.

Bob looked out the window. It was only ten o'clock on a rainy Monday, and he was already stressed out. His morning had started rather badly. First, there were the ten angry e-mails about the unfairness of a staff members' promotion, three phone calls regarding top management's lack of employee consideration of the new policy on vacation days, and two more phone calls about top management's lack of appreciation for an important assignment well done. Now two members of his team had stuck their heads in his office to ask what the point of their new job assignment was.

"Why does everyone here complain so much?" Bob muttered to himself. "It just doesn't seem like anyone is having any fun in this company, and that includes me. Maybe I can deal with it later. Let's just focus on solving some of these other problems so we can get through one more day."

But the unhappy people haunted him as his morning unfolded with the many tasks and interruptions of a busy day. Bob loved what he did and felt good about the work he and his team produced. For reasons he couldn't quite articulate, however, the work environment seemed to be getting more and more stressful and serious, and the employees were increasingly unhappy. *It's no fun*, Bob thought, and he realized that his employees knew it, too. In addition, he'd heard rumors that some of his key people were looking at other job opportunities. Engineering was a tight-knit professional community, and everyone knew everyone else's business.

Why am I looking forward to my lunch meeting with my Rotary Club so much? Bob wondered. *Why do I have so much fun there when I don't have it here? I thought it would be so fulfilling when I was promoted to district manager, that I could make people's lives better, that I would make great decisions that positively impacted the people working for me.* Then, it had looked like it would be satisfying to manage this office. He had looked forward to inspiring a team of highly skilled and competent engineers to do things that benefitted both the environment and the company and made them feel good about doing their jobs well. *But nobody seems happy about anything we do here,* he thought. *I don't understand it. We hire great people, we pay well, the benefits are terrific, and the work is really stimulating for our well-trained engineers.*

Well, it certainly hasn't worked out to be as much fun or as rewarding as I had hoped it would be, Bob reflected. *Oh, well,* he thought, *Lunch is almost here, and then I'll be free for a little while from all these unhappy people who seem to do nothing but complain all day about every little thing.* Didn't they know it wasn't his fault? What did they expect him to do? Sighing to himself, he straightened his tie and left the office.

When Bob arrived at the Rotary Club meeting, he sat down at a table with three other members he knew well. After the president called the meeting to order, she asked about members' announcements. Bob's friend Johanna stood up and issued a call for volunteers for an art festival the club was sponsoring that would benefit a local youth sports program. Next, Marshall stood and announced that the Habitat for Humanity project the club supported was going to have a workday at the job site that weekend. Finally, Alexis announced that she was in charge of a committee to organize a wine tasting and was looking for volunteers. Bob considered all three to be wonderful opportunities to do things he enjoyed and finally decided to help Johanna with the art festival. He was especially interested in athletic opportunities for youth, and he knew that this program meant a lot to the many children involved.

Bob was feeling pretty good about himself and his club. Here he could not only do worthwhile things, but he could do them with people who enjoyed doing them as much as he did, and they all were grateful for each other's fellowship. He had fun working on these projects with these people.

A few minutes later, Dr. Ken Berry, the speaker for the day, was introduced. Bob learned that the speaker, a medical doctor, had a reputation as a noted expert on "laugh therapy." *Boy*, he thought, *I sure could use some of that in my job.* As the speaker talked about the benefits of laughter, a provocative question struck Bob: *Why do I laugh and have fun here, where I voluntarily participate, while I don't have fun at my job, where I'm paid to be?*

Afterward, Bob joined the line of those wanting to meet the speaker and get an autographed copy of his book, *It Only Takes a Minute to Put Some FUN in It. Being last in line has its advantages*, Bob thought. *Maybe Dr. Berry has some ideas.*

As Dr. Berry was signing his book, he looked up at Bob, and said, "So, Bob, are we having fun yet?" Bob was stunned. It was the very same question that had started his day at the office. "Well, actually, no," Bob replied.

Bob went on to say that Dr. Berry's presentation about the benefits of laughter had inspired him to think a lot about the work setting at his organization. "Not only is no one at my office laughing and getting those benefits, but no one is even having fun," he explained. It was almost as if there was a sign on the wall proudly proclaiming "243 consecutive days without the interference of laughter."

"So you're not having fun at work, but you'd like to?" Dr. Berry asked.

"Of course," Bob answered. "Anyone would. I want my team to have more fun, too. I actually think we'd be more productive. At the very least, we wouldn't always be so stressed out. I just don't know where to start.

"Dr. Berry, would you have time for a cup of coffee? I would love to find a starting point for something like this."

"Well," said Dr. Berry, "first, call me Ken. Second, I don't have time today, but I do have some time tomorrow morning. Let's meet at 10 a.m. at the Koinonia Kafe on Martin Drive. Do you know the place?"

"Yes, of course," Bob replied.

"Great, I'll see you there," said Ken. "Meanwhile, I've got some homework for you. Stop by the Changing Hands Bookstore. See what you can find on fun and humor at work. Let me know what you find tomorrow. Oh, and think about where in your life you are having fun right now. I'll see you then."

Back at the office, the question Bob had pondered during Ken's speech haunted him as he settled in to handle the complaints he had received that morning. Why did he have more fun in a volunteer organization than at his job where they paid him to work enthusiastically on the company's behalf? He actually paid the Rotary Club annual dues to get the fun and enjoyment that he should be getting out of working in his own organization. What was wrong with this picture?

This deserved further thought, and Bob spent several moments that afternoon reflecting on what he got out of Rotary and why it was fun. This was at least part of the answer to the assignment Ken had given him.

After work, he stopped at Changing Hands as Ken had suggested. He started examining some bestsellers in the management section. He picked up Ken Blanchard's *One Minute Manager, Gung Ho!* and *Leading at a Higher Level;* Tom Peters' *In Pursuit of Wow!,* Terrence Deal and M. K. Key's *Corporate Celebration*, and James Kouzes and Barry Posner's *The Leadership Challenge.*

Flipping though these books, he noted a repeated mention of the importance of having fun at work. One phrase by Kouzes and Posner caught his eye, "If you—and others—aren't having fun doing what you're doing, chances are people aren't doing the best they can do." He then picked up the more recent book by Dennis Bakke, *Joy at Work*, where he saw the point made even more strongly. Bakke argued that work should be fun, exciting, stimulating, and totally enjoyable. Another author, Karl Albrecht, in *The Power of Minds at Work: Organizational Intelligence in Action*, presented his belief that a sense of humor is one of the ten most important components of what he calls practical intelligence. Albrecht said good managers should ask themselves, "How well developed is my sense of humor?"

As Bob looked further through the shelves, similar sentiments seemed to pop out of a number of other books where respected practitioners and consultants described their managerial philosophies. Chili's former CEO Norm Brinker, in his book *On the Brink*, wrote, "If you have fun at what you do, you'll never work a day in your life. Make work like play—and play like hell." In the book *Nuts!*, Kevin and Jackie Freiberg described the type of people Southwest Airlines seeks to hire: "First and foremost, Southwest Airlines looks for a sense of humor … We look for attitudes; people with a sense of humor who don't take themselves too seriously … who work hard and have fun at the same time." The Freibergs discovered that Southwest believed that if it was to achieve its core principle of "Make flying fun" for its customers, it needed to make its employees' jobs fun first.

Boy, I've got plenty to talk with Ken about tomorrow, Bob thought.

The next morning, Bob was at Koinonia Kafe five minutes early. Ken was already there and stood to greet him. "Good morning. Are we having fun yet?"

Bob laughingly said, "No, but I've thought a lot about it since your talk yesterday."

"Let's get you a cup of coffee—and then you can tell me all about it." A few minutes later, Ken said, "So what have you found so far?"

Bob shared with him his thinking and what he had found in the bookstore.

"And if you were to boil it all down to a single sentence, what would it be?" Ken asked.

Bob thought a minute and then replied, "All these successful writers reinforce what I've learned working on service projects with my friends at Rotary—that it is important to have fun when you work."

"Very good," said Ken. "And what questions does that raise?"

A variety of provocative questions immediately surged through Bob's mind, and he started thinking out loud: "Why do I feel it's necessary to have fun? If this is true for me, might it be true for others, too? Maybe this is the missing ingredient in my own work setting. The challenge is how to create a fun work environment for me and everyone else. Does everyone see fun the same way? What is a fun work environment, anyway? What is it that makes employees feel they are having fun at work? If all these wise and successful people feel that fun is important, shouldn't I be considering what they are saying more closely? And all of this lines up with what you shared in your talk yesterday."

"Excellent," said Ken. "Go on. What is it that makes Rotary fun for you?"

Thinking further, Bob reflected back on what made his participation in Rotary so enjoyable. After a pause, he said, "I think there are three things. First, it's a sense of regularly coming together with like-minded people to do something worthwhile for the community and, by extension, for the world at large. The work I've done on service projects was not only fun, but it was also defined in everyone's mind as important. By being a part of this large service organization, I get the satisfaction of giving back something of value to my community—I think this is important and needed—and that makes me feel good. As a bonus, I do it with people I like. It really made the service projects fun.

"Second, the projects we complete are publicly commended by the club's leadership and by others in the community. It makes me feel good when we are recognized and applauded for our efforts. On occasion, the club president reads letters of gratitude to the club that are sent by recipients of its efforts. And the club is also recognized in the newspaper for its community contributions.

"Third, for some reason, I just feel better physically when I'm working with my friends on these worthwhile projects. Smiling, laughing, and joking while you work may not seem to be a big deal to some people, but to me it makes a difference in how I feel when I'm volunteering."

"Can you give me a specific example?" Ken asked.

"Of course," Bob replied without hesitation. "I know I had fun on our Habitat for Humanity project when we helped a family build its own home. And I always have fun on our international exchange programs when we bridge international boundaries with other countries."

"And what's missing from your job? Why don't you experience the same fun there?" Ken asked. "By performing well on your job, don't you contribute to building international relationships, provide jobs and opportunities for people worldwide who otherwise wouldn't have them, and make your community a better place?"

Bob had never thought of it that way before, and it stunned him. Why couldn't he introduce the same things in his workplace that he got from Rotary? He recognized

the contributions the company made to the community through what he and his co-workers did. Surely he could help them recognize what they were doing was worthwhile. Better yet, they got paid for it. "There must be something more I need to learn here," Bob said. "But what, and how?"

"Why do you think I asked you to put some thought into fun in the workplace and do a little research at the bookstore?" Ken asked.

"I don't know," Bob admitted. "I guess I hadn't thought about it."

"Well, one of the authors you mentioned earlier, Ken Blanchard, also co-authored a book called *Know, Can, Do.* In it, Ken quotes his wife, Margie, as saying the gap between knowing and doing is much greater than the gap between knowing and not knowing.

"I can't tell you how many people come up after my talks with the same questions you have. Most of them are looking for the next formula, the next fad, the next answer. They never stop to think about what they already know but aren't doing. Or that perhaps part or maybe all of the solution to their problem rests with them—and not the environment or other people. So, before meeting with anyone, I ask them to do some thinking and some research. If they do, I'm happy to continue to invest time with them. If they don't, we have a pleasant chat, a cup of coffee—and that's the end of it. So in a way, I was giving you your first test—and you passed with flying colors. Are you ready for the next step?"

"Yes, I am," Bob said as he smiled.

"It won't be that difficult," Ken said. "I want you to talk with some people whom you probably already know. But each of them has a piece to the puzzle you're trying to solve. Do you know Ed Evans and Juanita Aguilera?"

"Of course," Bob said. "They're both in my Rotary Club."

"And how would you describe the companies they work for?" Ken asked.

"They're fun places to work," Bob said without hesitation.

"And how do you know that?" Ken asked.

"Because of the conversations we've had," Bob answered.

"So, now I want you to call them and find out why they're fun," Ken said. "Then, we'll meet again."

When Bob got to his office, he opened his address book and looked for the phone

numbers. Ed worked at All Region Electric, the power company, and Juanita worked at Whole Health Care Center, the area hospital.

With a sense of excitement and anticipation, Bob picked up the phone to call his friends to find out what they were doing to create a fun environment at their companies. As the receptionist was putting Bob's call through to Ed, he decided to start a list of these new insights. After thinking about his volunteer experiences with Rotary, he wrote the following conclusion on his office whiteboard:

INSIGHT #1: You can get a lot of people to do a lot of things, such as work on service projects, hold elective office, work longer hours, or donate money, if there is an element of fun.

INSIGHT TWO

Having Fun in a Serious Business

Can you have fun when work is no laughing matter?

"The workplace needn't be a salt mine, a galley ship, or a… mind-numbing, spirit-breaking experience."

—Ron Zemke

"The four signs of an effective corporate culture include the four Fs: focused, fast, flexible, and fun."

—Rosabeth Moss Kanter

"There ain't much fun in medicine, but there's a heck of a lot of medicine in fun."

—Josh Billings

Bob waited while the phone rang. His friend answered with a very friendly, "Hello, I'm Ed Evans. What can I do to make your day more successful?" Bob could almost see Ed's smile over the phone, and this made him smile.

"Ed," Bob said, after identifying himself, "I met with Ken Berry this morning. He asked who I knew who worked in a fun environment—the kind of environment I want to create for my people. Your name came to my mind. You mentioned how much fun you have working at the power company. I started wondering why I was having fun in a lot of other places, but not at work. I like my job and what I do, but for some reason the place where I work isn't very enjoyable."

"I know what you mean," Ed replied. "Several years ago, I felt the same way about this place. Today, as you know, it's changed 180 degrees. It seems like everyone enjoys not only what they are doing, but also the fact that they can do it here with each other. We do have a good time. By the way, it started with me having coffee with Ken Berry."

Bob laughed. "I should have guessed! I want to learn what you're doing so I can duplicate it here. I know if I'm not having much fun, the employees who work for me probably aren't either."

"Why not come over and visit us?" Ed offered. "I'll try to show you how we make this a fun place to do our jobs. Maybe some of it will spark some ideas."

"Great," Bob said. "How about tomorrow at 10 a.m.?"

"Terrific. I'll see you then."

The next day, Bob showed up at Ed's office. "Okay, here I am," Bob said with anticipation. "Tell me what goes on here that makes this a fun place to work."

"Well," Ed said, "you have to start by considering what we do and how we do it. This is a nuclear power plant, and the possibility of major problems is on our minds all the time. Indeed, when I came to work here, the tension was extremely high. People were pretty stressed out. No one was having any fun, although it was a very challenging and interesting job. With Ken's help, I decided we needed to find a way to take some of the stress and tension out of this place. It really started with an underlying philosophy that accents fun. We believed that people who are tense all the time will eventually burn out and, more importantly for what we do here, they won't pay as careful attention to their work as people who are relaxed and enjoying themselves while they do their jobs."

"So what did you do?" Bob asked. "Dress up in Halloween costumes? Throw water balloons? Lead a morning yoga routine?"

"We didn't really start with a defined and structured program," Ed explained. "We asked our staff how we could help them relieve their stress and make their jobs more fun. They had a lot of ideas, and we talked about them in a few team meetings. For example, we had to do things that wouldn't jeopardize the safety of the plant by doing something that would distract an operator who was monitoring critical gauges. Beyond that, anything was fair game, and boy, did these people come up with some creative ideas!"

"Sounds intriguing," Bob said. "Go on."

"Well," Ed continued, "the first thing we did was create a 'fun committee' where everyone was responsible for generating and introducing fun ideas. We wanted to go slow at first until we saw how the process worked. We have twelve people on our team, so each member was assigned one month of the year and was asked to come up with one fun idea for that month. Later, we gave them free rein to do this more frequently.

"That got them going. Even team members who had little interest in doing anything like this got into it, because they could invent something that made the job fun for them even if others thought it was a stretch. For example, our lead operator is José; he is Hispanic and proud of it. He figured it would be fun to get people to dress up for one day with something that was associated with their respective heritages. It was really interesting to see the diversity in my team. We had people wearing the Irish kelly green outfits next to those with serapes and even a person wearing a Scottish kilt. It gave people a chance to talk about their backgrounds a bit, and they seemed to enjoy having a different topic of conversation for that day."

"Another time, Vang, our secretary, held a Tai Chi session during our morning break. Nobody really understood it, but they seemed to have fun moving around in slow motion. Of course, it probably looked a little bit weird to some of our co-workers from other departments, but we've learned to live with that."

After pondering that mental image, Bob asked thoughtfully, "What happens if someone doesn't want to do whatever it is the fun committee leader introduced for that month?"

"Easy," Ed responded. "We all agreed at the beginning that if someone didn't want to participate, no one would force it. This was one of Ken's principles. This agreement up front did two really important things for all of us. First, it gave people the right not to participate. That in itself is a wonderful message of respect for individual differences. Second, it started a healthy competition among our team members to find things that many people will do. They compete against each other to see who can get the most people to join whatever it is they are doing for their day. It becomes a very competitive game. I've seen some pretty inventive things put on the table, but more importantly, the employees on my team seem to spend more time thinking about and investigating what each person likes and doesn't like and then finding things that everyone will feel good about doing. If part of a fun work environment is feeling good about the people you work with, this idea seems to be paying off for me and my team in a big way.

"One final benefit we get from this team-directed fun is that it encourages creativity in other areas of employees' work responsibilities. One difficulty of this job is encouraging people to be creative while at the same time paying attention to details and sticking to necessary routine safety protocols. Here, once a year, each member is challenged to find something that is fun for all, and they really stretch their minds on what they come up with. Best of all, they apply their creativity to their jobs, as well."

Bob thought about this a bit and then asked, "So you got your people to come up with fun ideas and that changed the work setting from dreary to fun? That seems like a lot of benefit from such a simple idea."

"That's just part of it," Ed said. "We do other things, as well, but the secret is simple for us. We work in a high-reliability power plant where no one but a few nuclear regulatory inspectors and a few corporate executives ever visit. I guess you could say that we could almost work in our pajamas here, and no one would really care. Obviously we don't do that, but the point is that we can do a lot of things that other companies may not be able to get away with. For example, we encourage employees to put some of their favorite cartoons on the wall, and they often adapt them by changing the captions or by labeling one of the characters with a colleague's name. It's all done in fun and good taste, of course," Ed said as he pointed to a large collection of *Dilbert* cartoons on the wall. "These are actually great communication devices for me, as well. I know something is bugging my team when I start to see cartoons on a particular topic showing up on the wall.

"I recall one cartoon that popped up when our plant was facing some quality and safety challenges, and the employees were concerned about whether it would close down. I'm a big football fan, and one of my team members found a picture of me in front of a TV set with a major scowl on my face as I was watching my favorite team lose. That picture has showed up in the oddest places ever since. The team even got a coffee mug made with that picture on it and slipped it on my desk one morning. I got a big kick out of it. The message was clear that we all occasionally have something to scowl about, and we need to share that pain. However, we can do so in a funny way. Maybe it's the equivalent of gallows humor, but it got everyone chuckling and made the situation more bearable. It seemed to take a lot of the tension out of the air.

"We do a lot of other things, too," Ed continued. "One person suggested we allow each member to customize his or her workspace as long as it wasn't dangerous, detrimental to the work function, or offensive to others. So we tried it. Some did it, and some didn't. I'll show you a couple of the more creative ones later. I found that customizing workspaces allowed some people one more avenue to show their creativity. We look for things that playfully keep our minds limber and our skills sharp without interfering with any of our critical job tasks and responsibilities. After all, I don't want an employee deciding that today is the day he is going to experiment on safety valve settings to see what is more effective.

"This job can be pretty boring, monitoring meters and gauges all day long. When it gets really exciting is when the needles go to red zones. Then it's 'Katie, bar the door,' and all of my team members get busy—and serious—very quickly.

"In other words, I have some really smart, well-trained people here whose training is not used very much, thank goodness. But when we need it, boy, is it important! I have to keep their minds engaged when they are not busy solving problems or fixing a mess. The little creative activities are one way we keep people active, alert, and having fun while we wait for the inevitable crises to occur.

"We have some other things we do to keep their minds engaged and active, as well, but you might not think of them as 'funny ha-ha' types of things. For example, we have an online program that simulates a nuclear power plant. This allows employees to practice anticipating and handling big problems in a virtual setting so when they see the real thing, they are ready. Plus, if you want to think of it this way, it's sort of like a big computer game for grown-ups. It's challenging, interesting, full of surprises, and we can set it up so we can have a contest to see who handles meltdowns the best. Mike over there is currently our 'Fishin' King'—get the pun? Fishin' and fission?— anyway, he won last month's challenge. His reward was the traveling trophy on his desk for a month—a singing Billy Bass with a fake mushroom cloud over his head. The team members like the simulation; they believe it's great practice for the real thing, and it keeps us all focused on what we are here to do.

"We also like to recognize professional achievements. Even if we don't often need to utilize our people's extensive skills, when we do need them, they are really vital. We want our engineers to feel we value their skills and their continuing development. Jamal got his Professional Engineering certification recently, and I got the company to spring the funds for a nice dinner at a classy steak house. It cost us a bunch, but it's worth it to tell the employees we value them as professionals and truly respect their expertise. I know I feel better about where I work when they make an extra effort to

tell me they appreciate me. I don't know if that is enough to make a place fun, but I figure it's one more thing that helps our people smile when they think about work instead of dreading coming here every day.

"During the slow times, we also promote opportunities for personal growth. We had a few people who organized a book club and a few others who put together a high-tech-oriented investment club. As a matter of fact, I invested a few thousand bucks into that venture, and most of the original members are still at it. We figure anything we can do to help our people grow and develop is worth doing. Not only do they enjoy it, but also we get the benefits of it. It makes me feel good when someone goes out to look at one of our competitors' plants and comes back saying, 'Wow, those guys have no fun at all!'

"We also found that reducing stress contributes to a more pleasurable work setting. Some of the fun things we do here release stress and the negatives associated with that. Let me give you two examples. We added a weight and exercise room two years ago and, much to my boss' surprise, it has been used a lot. I find when some people get totally frustrated with what they are doing, they go to the exercise room and work out. The physical exertion seems to have a positive effect on their attitude towards the work, as well. It may be something like the runner's high we read about except that it happens right here where we all can benefit from the employee blowing off some steam in a safe way.

"We also encourage our employees to participate in local philanthropic and service organizations. Like I told you earlier, we are always concerned about them keeping their mental edge, and so we try to give them opportunities to stay sharp. If they are encouraged to participate in things like our Lions Club or Kiwanis, they come back to work stimulated and invigorated. The opportunity to meet and talk with people who are not doing the same thing they are gives their minds a bit of a workout. It's a wonderful change of pace from the routine work of this business. It seems people like working environments that encourage and expect them to stay mentally active. Therefore, anything we can do to support that seems to pay off not only in the direct benefits that the community gets, but also in the benefits we get by having people come back to work refreshed and renewed. Maybe all work and no play, especially when the work is routine, does make Johnny or Jillian a dull person! Besides, you'd be amazed at what interesting new ideas we get around here from our employees talking to people who are not in our industry. We changed our whole method for training new employees based on what one person learned while working on a Habitat for Humanity project.

"Now," Ed concluded, "note that we haven't changed the nature of the jobs around here at all. What we have really focused on is the context around the employees' jobs. We recognize that even the most stimulating job containing the classical elements of autonomy, skill variety, task significance, task identity, and feedback will not produce satisfied workers if their surroundings are not palatable to them. So part of our rationale for adding a lot of fun activities is to create a job environment that is consistent with, and supportive of, the underlying job content. In short, an important part of my job is to manage the context for my employees to make it more satisfying to them."

After a quick tour of some of the more creative cubicles, Bob felt he had gotten a lot of good ideas. He thanked Ed and left. "I'm beginning to see what it means to have a fun work environment," he said to himself. He called Ken and arranged to meet for coffee again.

"So, I understand you met with Ed," Ken said after they both had coffees in hand.

"Yes, I did," Bob answered. "But you didn't tell me that you knew him—and that you had actually mentored him."

"I figured that would come out soon enough," Ken replied. "What was most important is that he was someone you knew and that you felt he worked in a fun environment. A consultant friend of mine has some laws of learning; and one of them is 'People don't argue with their own data.' It was a lot easier for you to learn from Ed because you had already identified that he had something you wanted. So what did you learn from Ed?"

Bob shared the list of the things he saw at the power plant and classified them into five categories:

1. Time off to participate in voluntary community activities
2. Actions that lower tension and loosen people up
3. Opportunities for employees to expand their work-related and personal talents
4. Opportunities to participate in friendly games like the simulation and quasi-athletic events
5. Humor (surprise, incongruity, jokes, quips, gags, puns, cartoons)

"Excellent," Ken said. "And what does that give you?"

"I see pieces of a 'fun tool kit' that I can use in my own organization," Bob said excitedly. "And I have a new insight from Ed to add to my whiteboard back at the office:"

INSIGHT #2: Most people want to have fun while also doing meaningful and productive work.

"You're well on your way," Ken said. "Let's get together after you've met with Juanita."

INSIGHT THREE

HAVE YOU HEARD THE ONE ABOUT...?

Having Fun When Everyone Is Watching

Can you have fun when clients are on-site?

"Humor, play, and fun make people more disclosing, uninhibited, participative, joyful, informal, expressive, spontaneous, genuine, authentic, optimistic, convivial, energetic, enthusiastic, and emotionally buoyant."
—Terrence M. Deal and M. K. Key
"We don't laugh because we're happy; we're happy because we laugh."
—William James
"The human race has one really effective weapon, and that is laughter."
—Mark Twain

As Bob headed to work the next day, he pondered how to apply what he had learned from Ed. *I suppose I could just go and replicate the five types of things that Ed is doing. But I wonder,* he thought, *if everything that works for Ed fits all types of organizations. We are a little different than a power plant because we meet daily with clients, have visitors in our offices a lot, and have to look professional at all times. After all, we are a professional engineering firm, and I suspect that not everything Ed can do inside his walls can be done in my company without scaring away our customers or at least making them wonder if we know what we are doing.*

Maybe I should also visit Juanita at the hospital and get a bigger picture before I do anything. Their operation is more like ours, since they perform their jobs in front of a very vigilant audience—their patients—who are constantly monitoring their professionalism. Following this reasoning, Bob called up Juanita at the hospital.

"Juanita," he said when she answered the phone, "you told me how great your work setting was when we chatted the other day. Both you and Ed Evans were telling me you had decided to make your workplaces fun. I talked with Ken Berry, our Rotary speaker, after his talk. What he said deepened my commitment to make my workplace more enjoyable. I want to see what you've done.

"I've already visited Ed, and I learned a lot. I'm wondering if you are doing the same things that Ed is. I'm guessing that what you do with all these patients watching might be quite different than what Ed can do behind his power plant's security fences. Can I come by and see what it is you do to make your place fun?"

Juanita laughed. "I was sure you'd connect with Ken. I did the same thing a year ago. It was his coaching that helped us make the changes that you're asking about. And, like Ed, I'm committed to 'paying it forward,' if you will. I'd love to show you what we're doing. Can you come over tomorrow?"

"I'll be there," Bob said.

When Bob walked into the hospital the next day, to his surprise, he could feel what he felt when he walked into Ed's power plant—a sense that it was a fun place to work. *It's odd,* Bob thought, *how you can tell almost immediately what kind of place it is when you walk in the door. People are smiling here, too, just like at the power plant. I hope I can figure out how this happens so I can make it work for us, too.*

Juanita greeted him with a friendly smile. "Welcome, Bob. Good to see you! I think what you are trying to do is great, and I am glad to help you," she said.

Bob looked at her thoughtfully. "What I learned from Ed," he said, "is that while his well-trained people had interesting jobs they liked doing, the previous work setting wasn't any fun to be in. Ed explained to me how he had created a more fun ambience to provide a positive work environment for his staff. What a difference it made to both his team and the company in a variety of positive ways!

"It seems to me that in some respects, the jobs your people do are similar to Ed's, but the work setting is very different. Your staff works in plain sight of everyone. Patients interact with them all day long and watch everything they do. If a nurse does something silly or acts in the playful ways that Ed's team does, wouldn't that jeopardize the faith of the patient in the skills of the nursing staff? After all, if the health care providers act unprofessionally, I expect patients would wonder, 'Do they really know what they are doing?'"

Juanita responded, "You're right, of course. We need to walk a fine line here. Our public is always watching us to see what we are doing and feeling. They have a big stake in what happens here, and most of them are relatively clueless about the sophisticated medical parts of what is going on. We discovered that they look for cues from us about their health status. If they think we are acting silly around them without a valid reason, then they might think we're not serious about their care or worse, are being careless and not paying attention to patient safety. On the other hand, interestingly enough, if we act too seriously, they may jump to the unrealistic conclusion that their health problems are worse than they really are or that their condition is terminal. We have to act in ways that don't communicate something to the patient that isn't true or is misleading.

"But that doesn't mean we can't make this a fun place to work. Like Ed's team, our staff also is under a fair amount of stress, but it's a different type of stress. I suspect," Juanita laughed, "that almost everyone feels that his or her job is stressful. Our staff, however, feels like it is such a life-and-death work environment that if we didn't have a way to relax and relieve the stress, we would be grouchy and tense all the time and, I think, not terribly effective. It is hard to be upbeat with a patient when you're not upbeat with your co-workers or yourself. Ever notice how irritability is contagious? If we have one person who is having a bad day, it is amazing how that rubs off on everyone else—both patients and staff. We learned long ago that we have to make sure we catch grumpiness in its early stages, or we will soon have an epidemic of grouchiness. I guess since we are a health care environment, we have to find ways to inoculate our staff against the grouchy germ. Having fun doing one's job is a good way to fight that nasty disease."

Bob listened to all of this and asked, "So what do you do to have fun if you can't do anything too visible or upsetting to the patient?"

Juanita laughed again and said, "It's not really that difficult. We try to find things that not only brighten our day and add a little playful variety to it, but also do things our patients can enjoy and even participate in, as well. After all, we know from the medical research that laughter really is good medicine. Consequently, when we encourage our own employees to do things that make them laugh, we are aiding the healing of our patients, as well. That's a pretty good two-for-one benefit, don't you think?"

Bob readily agreed, but he still wondered what they actually did. So he asked her again.

"Well," said Juanita, "come with me and I'll show you some of the things we do to promote a fun work setting."

Bob followed her to the orthopedic surgical ward. As they got off the elevator, there were balloons everywhere. Streamers hung from one side of the hall to the other, and a big sign read, "Happy Birthday, Samantha."

"What is that all about?" he asked.

"That's our birthday celebration for Samantha Carlson, a patient who turned 85 today," Juanita explained. "She had hip transplant surgery yesterday. Our admissions data manager is pretty clever and makes note of patient-oriented data like special birthdays and tells us about it. When we learned that today is Samantha's eighty-fifth birthday, we decided to have a celebration with cake and ice cream and all the hoopla. Everyone on the floor is invited to sing 'Happy Birthday' and share the cake. Patients are not forced to come, but we do make a special effort to include those who aren't mobile but want to be a part of it anyway. Because it is their choice, we get no complaints. It's a little extra work for us, but we find that many patients like the idea of celebrating something while they are here, a place where they'd rather not be. Here in the hospital, patients are closely monitored in a bed and assisted until they can go home. They are often scared and helpless, totally dependent upon others to take care of them. But they are also bored.

"A celebration does two things really well. First, it gives the patients some excitement in an otherwise pretty mundane routine. Second, it gives our nursing staff a chance to lighten up without being criticized for it by the patients. After all, they are staging a fun event for the benefit of the patient, so who can complain about that?

"From a customer service standpoint, it also gives us a tremendous amount of positive word-of-mouth publicity. Most people have no idea if their health care is really good or not, so it's the little celebrations like this that they talk about when they go home. We also take an instant photograph when each patient is discharged and give it to them to carry with them. On that day, most patients have huge smiles on their faces, so they are more likely to remember the positive side when they look back on their photo in the future.

"You should see our customer satisfaction ratings," she continued. "We know from the comments that doing things like this helps make the place fun for everyone and provides tangible evidence that we care. You may not immediately know if your surgeon inserted the artificial hip properly during surgery, but you remember the really fun events during recovery. We even go so far as to have a professional harpist in

here to play now and then. It gives the mobile patients a goal to walk to the recreation area as part of their therapy, and, for those who are still recovering, the relaxing music seems to soothe the soul. We find that entertainment is good for everyone. I picked that up on a trip to Disney World, where I talked to an employee who was singing along backstage with the music while working on the *Lion King* show. It hit me then that it's hard to be unhappy when you're singing a happy song.

"Our work is very demanding and challenging and important. Our staff loves the nursing profession. Just ask any one of them. They know what they do makes a real difference to our patients, and they are very proud of that. On the other hand, we discovered that the labor market for nurses is so tight that we needed to find a way to enhance our retention by making sure our nursing staff felt good about working here. We asked ourselves how we could make our hospital the employer of choice if a nurse could get the same salary for the same job at any of three hospitals in town.

"People who are doing their jobs in a place they feel is fun aren't as likely to quit. It's as simple as that. Show me one person who has 'too much fun' in his or her life, and I'll show you a genetically grumpy person I don't want to work with. If we want people doing their jobs with smiles on their faces, then we have to make sure they are having fun while they are under our roof. If we don't do it, our competitors will. Quite frankly, we have worked hard to make sure our competitors have to settle for the grouchy applicants while making sure our employees are having too much fun in their jobs to leave. So far, it's working pretty well. Our turnover rate is half that of our competition. More importantly, our absenteeism rate is much lower than our competitors', so we have to use fewer temporary nurses or fill-ins.

"These things just have a way of compounding," Juanita explained. "We discovered, for example, that the more temporary nurses we used, the lower the levels of both customer satisfaction and full-time employee satisfaction. The contract people are well trained, but they don't always care about our team culture or have the same commitment to our organizational values that our full-timers do. They're not a permanent part of our team, and everyone knows it. They don't participate in our socials, know the rules to any of our games, or care about celebrating the successes of our full-timers. Consequently, the fewer temporary employees we use, the more fun everyone has—patients and full-time employees alike.

"We do one more thing to cut down on temporary nursing. We have contests for attendance, and we do it in several different ways. We have team attendance awards and celebrations, and we have individual awards. By reminding the staff of how

important it is for them to be here, we strive to make them aware of their obligations to us, our mission, and each other as part of a patient-care team. After all, we're no different than any other organization. If people aren't here regularly, how can they feel part of our team or organization?

"It's a bit like our attendance commitment to our Rotary Club, but on a much grander scale," Juanita continued. "Recently, one team, which had perfect attendance from everyone on it, got a weekend getaway for all the team members and their families to a beachside resort. It was great fun, and the more they talk about it back at work, the more incentive it provides for the other teams to achieve the same level of attendance in the future. It's a fun and positive way to make sure our people are here to work and feel part of our organization. After all, what makes you feel good about an organization? Part of that is feeling you have an integral role in what the organization does. You have to be there often enough to be part of that. When we can get people to feel good about being here and then make them feel even better because we recognize they are here, we get a lot more smiles than you might think.

"We make sure we publicly recognize and show our appreciation for our perfect-attendance people and our longtime employees. After all, if employees have been with us for many years and are models of what we want our new employees to look like, why wouldn't we celebrate their time with us in a very public way? Not only are we appreciating their longevity, but we also send a powerful message to other employees about what type of person finds the hospital such a great place to work. Of course, you have to be careful that the longtime employees aren't turkeys or grouches, but that is an issue for our human resources department to deal with, and they do. My point here is that if you have good people and they like the place enough that they come and stay many years, then you need to make sure that the newer employees think about why these really good employees have stayed so long, rather than look for a job somewhere else.

"In short, fun work environments cut down on turnover and make hiring easier. Who would you like to work for—a company where everyone you meet is scowling or one where everyone is smiling? It doesn't take a rocket scientist to see the value of a fun work setting. Whatever we spend on pins, awards, and food, we make up for many times over in reduced turnover costs, fewer complaints, fewer legal problems, and reduced costs of employment. The word of mouth we have among nurses here in town is terrific. It sure makes my job easier and, I might add, that makes me smile more, too."

Bob asked, "What else do you do besides hold birthday parties for patients? Surely that doesn't do it all by itself. How much cake can one nurse or one patient eat, anyway—especially in this era of increased attention to healthy diets?"

Juanita laughed. "Don't worry, Bob. The celebrations are only the tip of the iceberg. We have team meetings before each shift starts where we talk about patient feedback. Good feedback means the patient felt good about the quality of treatment and personal care he or she received. Remember what I said earlier: most people have no idea if their health care was good or bad, but they sure can tell you if their experience here was good or bad by the way they were treated. We regularly read the patient letters, both good and bad ones, to our staff so they can feel the happiness, or the occasional unhappiness, our patients experience by being here.

"As I said earlier, our staff feels good about their profession because they really believe that they make a substantial difference for the patients they work with. When we tell them how much they are appreciated by those patients, they also feel good about being a part of our organization. It is a wonderful recognition of the care we give. If you believe your job is to give high-quality medical care, and a recipient of that care takes the time to write a letter to management describing how good that care was, don't you think having that read in a team meeting would make you feel good? Knowing how much your organization appreciates the good things you do surely makes for a more fun work setting than one in which no one ever notices."

Bob thought about that one and ruefully remembered all the times he hadn't bothered to mention some exceptionally good service experience he'd had and, worse yet, hadn't bothered to tell one of his own staff what a difference he or she had made in satisfying a customer. *A simple "Thank you and well done!" goes a long way to show appreciation*, he thought. *To work in a setting where management takes the time to express its appreciation, sincerely and publicly, is certainly a characteristic of an enjoyable place to be.*

"We also do a lot of fun social events for our team members away from the eyes of our patients," Juanita continued. "We feel a strong bond among us, and by getting together and having a pizza party after work, or an annual dinner dance, we get a chance to be together when the spotlight is off. More importantly, these nurses have been through some pretty traumatic experiences that only other people who have experienced the same things can relate to. We've found that by hosting these kinds of social events, we give them a chance to blow off some steam and talk through tough issues with others who understand because they've been there and know what they are going through.

"Buying a few pizzas and a case of soft drinks is pretty cheap from our standpoint. We like to combine these with public recognition banquets that are celebrations of achievements for individuals and for the hospital itself. When we got on the list of America's top 100 hospitals, we had a terrific celebration and gave gifts to commemorate the event. It was great. Our CEO stood in front of all 1,500 employees and said, 'YOU did it.' The glow of pride around here for the next few weeks was tangible. In fact, you can still feel some of it as you walk around here today because management has done a good job of reminding people how important this ranking is and how important they are in achieving this distinction. Now you even hear some of our employees talking about our facility making the top 10 list someday. If you don't think that helps make this a fun place to work, then you are not listening to what I am telling you.

"In other words, I've learned that there are as many ways to build a fun work setting as there are people who work in that environment. While it is likely that each one of them will tell you something different, we try to build in enough different things that everyone will find something that makes working here not only professionally rewarding, but fun, as well. The professional challenges of our staff's work provide the rewarding content in their jobs, but it's my job to make sure they are working in an environment or setting that allows them to have fun at the same time. I really believe that is why they want to stay here and not go to our competitors."

That afternoon, Bob called Ken to schedule another appointment. "Coffee at the usual place on Monday?" Bob asked.

"I think it's time I see where you work," Ken replied. "Why don't I come over at 11 a.m.? Does that work for you?"

"I'll make it work," Bob responded.

On Monday morning, Ken arrived a few minutes early. As they sat in a couple of comfortable chairs in front of Bob's desk, Ken looked around the office. As he saw Bob's whiteboard, he said, "I can see that you're taking this seriously, but are you having fun yet?"

Bob laughed, "I'm having fun learning. And I'm putting things together that I'm pretty sure will work here. I'm taking my time to really think things through, though. After all, you only get one chance to make a good first impression. I really want this to work."

"That's good thinking," Ken said. "So what did you learn from your visit to Juanita, and how does it compare with your visit with Ed?"

"Juanita does some of the same things Ed did at the power plant. However, the presence of patients creates a different work setting that made some things Juanita does to create a fun work environment more effective and desirable than what Ed did—at least as it applies to our company."

"And what does she do differently?" Ken asked.

Bob explained, "I've identified five new categories of fun activities from Juanita's hospital I can add to the five from Ed's power plant:

1. Recognition of personal milestones like employee birthdays or anniversaries.

2. Ice cream socials, high teas, pizza parties, and dress-up or costume days.

3. Special events to acknowledge and celebrate professional accomplishments.

4. Bringing in musical groups, artists, and entertainers to break the monotony.

5 Friendly competitions among employees and groups of employees.

"Juanita showed me there are many different activities management can utilize to create a fun work context for employees with challenging jobs. The combination of job content and context that pays off is having fun while working hard and still being professional. The secret is finding that unique set of activities that fits best with your work setting and your people. Although there are general categories of things that people find to be fun, the devil, and the real fun, is in the details."

"Good work!" Ken exclaimed. "So what can you add to your whiteboard?" Bob thought a moment and then added this:

INSIGHT #3: A wide range of activities exist that can provide fun even in serious work environments.

INSIGHT FOUR

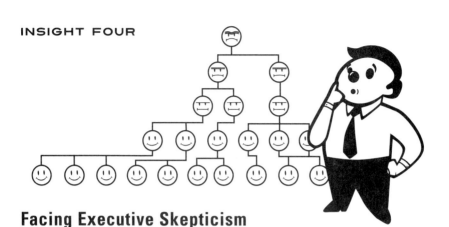

Facing Executive Skepticism

Do executives think fun is appropriate?

"Most workplaces are toxic energy dumps."
—Stephen Lundin
"People need to learn that they can have fun while being productive."
—Jack H. Llewellyn
"Laughter is the sun that drives winter from the human face."
—Victor Hugo

Bob was really getting enthused now. Ken was a great mentor, and he had picked up a lot of ideas from Ed and Juanita, but it was going to take some money in his budget to implement them properly. For that, he needed the support of his boss, Monika. He called Monika's secretary to set up an appointment to talk about having more fun at work. Monika's secretary, Sydney, upon hearing the subject for the meeting, was more than a little bit skeptical.

"Do you have any idea what you're talking about?" Sydney asked. "No one expects engineers to have fun, smile, or, God forbid, laugh."

Bob chuckled at Sydney's skepticism. "Please," he said, "we're not that serious are we?"

Sydney replied, "You know Monika, as well as I do. What do you think she'll say?"

Bob considered that a very good question and set about organizing his thoughts before meeting with Monika. He listed the ten categories contributing to a fun work environment that he had gathered in his two visits, and he reflected on which of those seemed to be the better fit for his team and his company.

Well, he thought, *certainly we can list the ten in an order that matches what kind of company we are. As a group of high-tech consulting engineers, we meet with a lot of professional people who are getting ready to spend a lot of money, and they depend upon our company for the kind of advice that will save them large sums of money. Our customers expect our advice to be perfect and don't hesitate to name us in lawsuits when they think it isn't. Our people are very skilled and well paid but are also under a lot of stress to meet deadlines with a perfect product. They are given incentives to be both accurate and fast, which is never easy to do. Over three-fourths of them have their Professional Engineer designation, and that is very prestigious in this business. I guess if I were to rank the ten categories of things I've discovered that make the workplace fun for us, I'd list them in this order:*

1. Public celebrations of professional achievements
2. Recognition of personal milestones
3. Fun social events
4. Humor
5. Games, including simulations
6. Opportunities to engage in volunteerism
7. Stress-relief activities, like the workout room
8. Entertainment, like the harpist at the hospital
9. Friendly competitions, such as Juanita had for attendance
10. Opportunities for personal growth

Well, Bob thought, *this should be a fairly easy sell to Monika, since we already do some of this anyway. We have our annual recognition day when we gather together to announce the achievements and accomplishments of our people and of the company itself. We also use that time to recognize people for longevity and give them their service pins. However, I don't think we do any of this very well. No one ever wants to go to these things, including the people getting recognized. But at least we do something. We also have some social events, an exercise room, a company softball team, and the company pays my dues to Rotary. It looks like we do several of these things already. If this is true, why isn't our place*

as much fun to work in as Ed's and Juanita's companies? Is there something I'm missing here?

He concluded there were two things missing. First, his organization did only a few of these things, and they did them infrequently. It was hard to feel like your professional achievement meant much when it was recognized along with thirty other people, half of whom were being given retirement gifts. A mass-production recognition ceremony left everyone with a bad taste in their mouth. The second explanation was that Monika simply wasn't known as a fun person. She seldom smiled and never joked. She appeared very serious all the time, and this sent a very strong message that she thought work was a serious endeavor. She was not the type of person you'd look to for leadership on creating a fun work environment. Nonetheless, Bob was determined to at least give it a try.

The next morning, Bob went to Monika's office. Monika glanced up from reading the advance memo Bob had sent her and looked at him with a puzzled expression. Then she asked pointedly, "What is all this about? Are you trying to tell me having fun is more important than being productive?"

Ouch, Bob thought. *This is not a good start to this conversation.* Nonetheless, he plowed on. "No," he said, "that isn't why I'm here. But I've noticed that people in other organizations are having more fun than my team is, and I want to do something about that."

"Well," Monika replied, "isn't that part of why we pay you? What are you doing wrong if your people aren't enjoying their work?"

Now, clearly on the defensive, Bob said, "I guess I'm not explaining this well. I think I'm doing a pretty good job, and I think our people do their jobs very well. We certainly do well on budget goals, productivity, and customer satisfaction. But I've noticed that people in other organizations are always talking about how much fun their work environment is, and nobody on my team does. I want to create the same type of environment here—or an even better one—and I need your help to do it."

Monika looked at Bob skeptically. Bob could tell she was wondering if there was really any validity to his plan or if it was a waste of her time. "Well," she finally said, in her typically gruff and direct manner, "What exactly are you talking about, and what do you want from me?"

Bob figured this was his only chance to sell this idea to Monika, so he'd better get it right. He said, "My staff really likes the challenges and responsibilities of their work

assignments. In that regard, they are happy. On the other hand, I have been hearing the rumors of who is out looking for new jobs and why they are doing so. We pay our people well and our benefits are more than competitive, but from what I hear on the grapevine, our employees just don't think this is a fun place to work. They can do comparable professional jobs just about anywhere, and so they figure there must be more to a work life than the job itself. They want more. In talking to people at other companies, I think I have figured out what that 'more' is. I'd like your support and help to create a fun work context."

Bob could tell Monika was thinking about this brand-new idea and was clearly puzzled. "What are you talking about?" Monika said. "What do I need to do, or for that matter, what do you need to do to create a fun work environment here? What does it take? What does it look like? What is a fun work environment anyway? How do I know when I have a fun work environment, and what difference will it really make to me, to the company, or to those who work for us? I'm happy to listen to you, but I don't understand what you're trying to do or what it means. And I don't see how it will pay off in any tangible results."

Bob could see his work was cut out for him. "I've done a lot of thinking about what a fun workplace is," Bob began. "And here is what I've come up with:

A fun work environment is one in which a variety of formal and informal activities regularly occur that are designed to uplift people's spirits and positively and publicly remind people of their value to their managers, their organization, and to each other through the use of humor, playful games, joyful celebrations, opportunities for self development, or recognition of achievements and milestones."

Monika looked at him and asked, "Don't we already do that? We have an annual review process to recognize and reward achievements and accomplishments, an annual banquet to celebrate the milestones, and we sponsor a company softball team. What more do you want? Would you be happy if I gave you extra money in your budget for a few pizza parties?"

"Well," Bob replied, "that's a start, but I'm thinking that the key parts of this definition are the words 'variety of formal and informal activities' and 'regularly.' We have sort of fallen into the 'hold the annual assembly to read off the names' rut. No one takes it seriously, because it doesn't feel like management enjoys doing it. We need to do more—much more—to make this a fun place to work.

"When I visited my colleagues at other companies, I saw a lot of things they were doing that we could do to make working here more fun. For example, beyond the things we do annually, they hold contests that get people to pay attention to important parts of the job in a fun way instead of it being one more thing to do. My friend Ed at the power company gets his people to stay sharp on their power plant skills by using a simulation that gets everyone to compete against everyone else. It's like a big Pac-Man game for them, but it has a deadly serious purpose in training. People have fun and view this regular training regimen as something to look forward to instead of the drudgery some of our employees view annual update training to be. It's not a matter of getting better speakers; it's a matter of taking the time to make the training fun. They all know it's important and truly appreciate the fact that management knows that, too. More than that, management wants to make it part of the fun of doing the job instead of drudgery. Juanita from the hospital does the same thing by setting up little contests for attendance. It's important that the staff members are on duty so they reward that in a fun way instead of merely counseling them about poor attendance when they have a lot of absenteeism.

"When the power company meets an important safety goal, they have a party. When the hospital gets a thank-you letter from a patient, they have a party. These two managers are encouraged by their organizations to find ways to celebrate their people's successes and achievements. I don't think we are any different than they are in that our people also want to be recognized for their achievements and supported in their growth. We need to do more than our annual 'recognize everyone' event."

Monika said, "I'm afraid I don't see it. We're here to do our jobs. We pay our people well and give them competitive benefit packages to keep them satisfied. The jobs are challenging, and we hire people who like challenges. We don't have time to have parties or these other things. We devote enough of our budget to these kinds of activities now. If we put more money into doing more of them, it would have to come from somewhere. I don't see our people eager to give up salary dollars so we can spend more on awards, dinners, and plaques. At least I'm not, and besides, what will my boss say when I go to him and tell him I need a budget increase for balloons? Don't you think I will look a bit silly asking for party hats when our budget is tight anyway? I doubt anyone who works for you would come in here and support what you're saying. They don't care about this. All they care about is doing their jobs and getting paid well. They know we're all here to work and not play. Frankly, I am a little surprised that you're wasting so much time with this when you have work to do."

Bob knew he was in trouble now. Monika's concerns were valid. Monika hadn't seen Ed's power plant or Juanita's hospital and didn't know what a difference they both thought fun made in terms of productivity, employee morale, ease of hiring and retaining employees, and customer service. *It's hard to argue with someone who doesn't know what she doesn't know,* Bob thought. He knew he had an uphill battle to convince the doubting Monika. He thought maybe it was time to end this meeting and gather some information that might influence Monika to change her mind and support the idea of creating a fun work environment.

"Well," he said, "let me gather some more information. You ask very good questions about the benefits and value of creating a fun work environment. In my enthusiasm, I suspect I got a little ahead of myself in asking for your support, but I can get that information, and I will. I believe this is a good thing to do based on what I've seen, and I still want to pursue this further."

Monika looked at him and said, "Okay. You can chase this wild goose, but don't come back until you have some compelling evidence that this is worthwhile if you want my support."

Bob pondered the lesson learned from his meeting with Monika and formulated it as Insight #4. He wrote it down on the large whiteboard on his office wall to encourage others to ask questions about it.

INSIGHT #4: Fun at work is not historically viewed as an integral part of a manager's responsibilities. Consequently, it will not be easily accepted by superiors without compelling evidence.

INSIGHT FIVE

The Payoff from Fun at Work

Is there supporting evidence?

MAKE YOU FEEL GOOD
LOWER BLOOD PRESSURE
REJUVENATE
REDUCE STRESS
PROTECT THE HEART
BOOST THE IMMUNE SYSTEM
ELEVATE ONE'S MOOD

"Laughter is the best medicine."
> —*Traditional proverb, as used in* Reader's Digest

"When you have fun, you can do amazing things."
> —*Joe Namath*

"Time spent laughing is time spent with the gods."
> —*Japanese proverb*

Bob now realized it would take both rational arguments and considerable persuasiveness to get his boss to buy into the ideas that were bouncing around in his mind. He wondered if there was any evidence beyond the terrific testimonials he had received from Ed and Juanita that would help him sell the ideas to his skeptical boss.

Bob called Ken's office to see if he had any hard evidence that would help. After three rings, the answering machine kicked in with a highly unusual message. It began with a person laughing hard and trying to talk at the same time. Bob translated it as, "Leave a message, and we'll get back to you when we stop laughing."

Bob thought this was rather strange for a medical doctor, but after reflecting on it, he realized that it was actually an appropriate message for a person who gave speeches on the importance of humor. Obviously, Ken was a man of his beliefs. And it fit with Bob's experience with him personally.

A full day went by before Ken called him back. "I'm sorry for the delay in returning your call, but I was out of town for a speaking engagement, and I just returned," Ken apologized when he returned Bob's call. "What can I do to make your day a happier one?"

"Ken, everything I've done because of your prompting up to now has been great. But my boss Monika has been asking some tough questions I can't answer. I need to find answers if I'm going to be able to go full steam ahead with my 'fun at work' proposal." Bob told Ken about Monika's challenge to find some evidence that having fun does anything worthwhile and expressed the hope that he could get some help from Ken.

"Let's meet for lunch today, since I'm free then," suggested Ken. "We can talk about this some more."

Bob quickly agreed. They decided upon a place that was easy for both of them to find, and then selected a convenient time. When the hour arrived, Bob appeared at the restaurant to find Ken already there. "All week, I've been on a high since your presentation," he told Ken. "Meeting with you, talking to Ed and Juanita, all the notes I've taken. I thought everything would fall into place—but my boss Monika has a very different perspective. It nearly stopped me cold.

"Since yesterday I've thought about everything you said last week. I had gone to the Rotary meeting after a rather negative morning where everyone around me seemed to be unhappy. Hearing you and talking to my friends at Rotary got me thinking that it shouldn't be that way. I now think it's more important to be having fun and experiencing laughter than I had thought. I believe you when you say there are some important physiological, as well as psychological benefits from being happy at work. Unfortunately, my boss thinks this is highly questionable, so I need to find convincing evidence that creating a fun work environment is worth the time and effort. I'm not skeptical, but my boss is, and I need to speak with facts. My company is filled with engineers who don't believe anything unless it has some valid data behind it. Besides, I have to admit that it seems pretty simplistic to believe there is a causal relationship between fun and anything else that organizations value."

"Not a problem!" Ken said laughing. "Some of my best friends are engineers and some of them are even civil."

Bob winced at the bad joke but found himself chuckling anyway as he rapidly got into a more relaxed mental state. "I want to take this step by step. First, tell me what constitutes humor and how that ties in to the medical benefits of fun and laughter. I guess I should have asked that in our first meeting."

"Well, it's a form of communication," said Ken. "It can be a joke, pun, cartoon, story, gag, or almost anything that has either a funny intent or effect. On a more formal level, the Association for Applied and Therapeutic Humor defines it as 'any intervention that promotes health and wellness by stimulating a playful discovery, expression, or appreciation of the absurdity or incongruity of life's situations.' When you classify humor, you find that it often falls into the categories of teasing, misfortune, surprise, self-ridicule, nonsense, stupidity, or tales of clumsiness. The main things to avoid are ethnic, racial, or sexual stories; destructive or offensive language; or anything you wouldn't say directly to your mother. It's a good idea to test it on another audience, and then add it to your inventory of good material. If you're trying out a new story or gag, screen it carefully, keep it brief, and make sure it has a point or teaches a lesson. The best humor is truly memorable for its implications at work," he concluded.

"But let me move on to the effects of humor," Ken continued. "Simply put, when you are laughing, you feel better than when you are not."

"I believe that myself," Bob quickly replied, " but can I prove it or at least provide some supporting evidence to my boss that will back up what I think?"

"We certainly can," said Ken. "Let me tell you what we know about laughing and how it makes us feel better. Stop me if I get too technical, but I want to show you that there is strong evidence behind what I am telling you, and then I'll provide a physiological explanation for the benefits of fun."

With that, Ken reached into his pocket for a fact sheet. "Let me show you some information on the effects of laughter on people. This is based on some research done by Dr. Lee Berk of Loma Linda School of Medicine and Public Health. He found in one of his studies that the number and activity level of natural killer cells—such as gamma-interferon, T-cells, and B-cells, which are responsible for attacking viral and cancer cells—was increased after sustained and consistent laughter.

"There are other studies on the benefits of laughter for people. For example, we know that the amount of salivary immunoglobulin A, which protects the respiratory tract from infectious organisms, is increased after laughing. We also know that the negative physiological response to stress is reduced with laughter and that the levels of harmful epinephrine and dopamine are lower in groups exposed to humor.

"Now, let me simplify this," he continued. "What this all means, in lay terms, is that laughter reduces blood pressure, increases blood flow in the gastrointestinal tract, gives your diaphragm and other bodily muscles a workout, and reduces the sense of pain. In short, laughter stimulates the immune system and makes you feel better. How can you beat that?

"You see, a good belly laugh is kind of like taking your guts out for a jog. One researcher claims that laughing one hundred times a day is the equivalent of rowing for ten minutes. This researcher reports that laughter can increase the heart rate, improve blood circulation, and exercise muscles all over the body. How's that for a deal? You can get a good solid workout and not get sweaty doing it!

"In the late 1970s, Norman Cousins wrote his autobiography *Anatomy of an Illness*, which described his battle with ankylosing spondylitis, a chronic, inflammatory arthritis. He described how ten minutes of belly laughing each day helped him get two hours of pain-free sleep; medical scholars later researched the effects of laughter. After this book came out, more medical professionals became interested in what humor and laughter can do medically for people who are sick or want to avoid getting sick. Laughter has been credited with releasing endorphins, which are the body's natural painkillers and protectors against depression.

"Psychological benefits abound, too. In fact, laughter therapy is now a recommended approach used by mental health professionals all over the country," Ken continued. "That process teaches troubled people how to laugh in difficult situations. And professional study groups, such as the International Society for Humor Studies, have sprung up to conduct research on humor and laughter. We even have a name for this subspecialty of medicine; it's called gelotology—the scientific study of the body's reactions to humorous experiences."

Ken went on. "Do you remember the movie *Patch Adams*, starring Robin Williams and his famous red nose? Well, I've met Patch in person, and he really is as humorous as he was portrayed—even more so. What he does in the medical field certainly should be helpful in your company with a bunch of serious engineers. We know that laughter reduces stress in the workplace, rejuvenates employees, and changes their perspective and attitudes towards problems.

"Just think about it. Recall a situation when you were in a major crisis and you were able, by some fortunate bit of luck, to laugh during a moment of tension. Didn't you feel better? More relaxed? Have a different outlook on the situation you were in? Humor that produces laughter is as powerful a tool for managers as it is for doctors.

It offers a powerful distraction from physiological pain, so it stands to reason that it should offer an equally powerful distraction from psychological pain. It's hard to cry when you're laughing and hard to be mad at someone who's making you laugh. Better yet, I've found it to be contagious. Once one person starts laughing, it's amazing to see how easy it is to get others doing the same thing. Best of all, it's free. Medicare doesn't cover the cost of administering humor, but it doesn't matter."

"Here is a summary list of the benefits I've discovered through my careful reading of the medical literature. Basically, humor and laughter can:

- reduce stress,
- lower blood pressure,
- elevate one's mood,
- boost the immune system,
- improve brain functioning,
- protect the heart,
- improve personal connections with other people,
- rejuvenate,
- change perspectives and attitudes about problems, and
- make you feel good.

"That's a pretty impressive list, wouldn't you say?" Ken asked.

Bob was impressed and readily agreed. He had suspected all along that the old saying 'Laughter is the best medicine' was true; however, he hadn't realized how much research existed to support that. He had learned a lot from Ken and felt he had gathered some useful evidence to bring back to his boss.

Bob paid the bill, thanked Ken, and got up to go.

"Remember," Ken said, "laughter and humor are serious business. They offer real and demonstrable benefits to people. Why would anyone not want to see a fun work environment where people are encouraged to laugh? Tell your grouchy boss that it will save the company money on its health insurance. Maybe that will get her attention and support!"

Bob laughed and said good-bye. He headed back to his office on a natural high, feeling like he had made substantial progress in answering his boss' "So what?"

question. He was starting to find that fun and laughter did make a difference, an important one at that.

When Bob returned to the office, he wondered if anyone had documented the value of humor at work with substantive research data from real practitioners. He turned to his computer, and Googled "fun at work." Seconds later, he found that the Society of Human Resource Management had published a survey on the topic. He knew Madysen, the HR director, was a member of SHRM and decided to ask her if she had a copy.

A few moments later, he found Madysen at her desk. "Madysen, do you recall seeing the SHRM study on fun at work?"

Madysen looked up. "Why, Bob," she said, "are you looking to have some fun?"

"Right," Bob said in a jesting fashion, and then quickly turned the conversation back into a serious mode before he got into trouble. "Actually, I am looking for some information on how a fun workplace can aid a company and its employees. I have learned about the medical benefits of laughter, humor, and fun, but now I would like to find some data on the direct business benefits," Bob explained. "I'm trying to convince Monika we need to work on creating a more enjoyable and positive environment. Unfortunately, she thinks I'm nuts to spend time and energy on this. She was willing, however, to give me a chance to prove my point. She challenged me to find any information that supports the notion that having a fun work environment makes a difference, especially to the bottom line. So far, I've learned a lot about the physiological and psychological effects, so I know it benefits the individual, but I am still looking for evidence that it makes a difference to an organization."

"Look no further," said Madysen. "I can get that study for you. I'd be interested to see what benefits it holds for us, too. Maybe you're onto something that we can use across the company. I'll log into my SHRM account when I get a chance and print it off for you. Is Monday soon enough?" Bob said that would be great and headed back to his office, anxious to tackle his inbox.

Monday morning, as Bob was reaching for his new *Dilbert* mug, Madysen knocked on his door and poked her head in. "I have it," she said proudly. "Here is that SHRM study you wanted. I took a look at it myself, and it is really provocative. You must realize, of course, that a study of HR managers' opinions won't give you conclusive proof of anything, but nevertheless the data are still very intriguing."

After reading it, Bob decided it was time to see Ken again, so he called and set up a coffee appointment for the next morning.

"Good morning," Ken said as Bob arrived for coffee. "You look excited."

"I am," Bob replied. "After our last meeting, I got our HR Manager to help me with some research that SHRM had done. It was very interesting and reinforced the medical evidence you gave me for fun in the workplace."

"What did you learn?"

"Well," Bob said, "It reported on a nationwide survey of HR managers who were asked about the reasons for having fun at work and the benefits they saw from it. That group's responses showed that the apparent level of fun in most organizations is pretty low. Only a small minority of the HR managers thought the amount of fun was about right. Indeed, three-fourths of this group thought the level of fun their employees were having at work was less than what it ought to be. At the other extreme, only a paltry 3 percent indicated there was too much fun in their organizations."

"So, it appears that fun works. Pun intended," Ken said. "What else did you find out?"

"The report also included a wealth of specific ideas from the sampled HR managers about how to create a fun work environment like casual dress days, half-day Fridays, and candy-grams [Appendix 4]. The most frequently practiced types of activities they reported are those related to public celebrations of professional achievements and recognition of personal milestones. These were followed closely by the mention of fun social events. The HR managers felt there was considerable utility to be gained for both employees and the organization by providing fun activities at work. Finally, the HR managers recommended that all such activities should be utilized more frequently than they currently are."

"Pretty impressive," Ken said.

"I agree," Bob replied.

"So what are your conclusions?" Ken asked.

"Based on the study's data, I'd say these managers were saying there are many different ways to create a fun work environment. As an interesting aside, many of them highlighted the availability of free food."

Ken laughed and said, "So people really do like a free lunch!"

"I guess so!" Bob chuckled. "Beyond this, however, these HR managers believe that there were several other ways to create a fun work environment. It listed ten key categories of how to do this, which reiterated what I had discovered from Ed and Juanita."

"And what are they?" Ken asked.

"Here's my list, in order of frequency," Bob said as he took a piece of paper from a folder and handed it to Ken.

Ken read:

FIGURE 5-1
Categories for Fun-at-Work Activities

Recognition of personal milestones (e.g., birthdays and hiring anniversaries)

Fun social events (e.g., picnics, parties, and social gathering)

Public celebrations of professional achievements (e.g., award banquets)

Opportunities for community volunteerism (e.g., civic and volunteer groups)

Stress-release activities (e.g., exercise facilities and massages)

Humor (e.g., cartoons, jokes in newsletters and e-mails)

Games (e.g., training simulations, darts, bingo, and company-sponsored athletic teams)

Friendly competitions among employees (e.g., attendance and sales contests)

Opportunities for personal development (e.g., quilting class and book club).

Entertainment (e.g., bands, skits, and plays)

"So, what can you learn from this list?" Ken asked.

"For one thing, I can see that there are a lot of things that lead to a fun work environment. It's not a 'one-size-fits-all' approach. I can see why I enjoy my Rotary Club involvement so much. It relates to the fourth item on the list: the opportunity

to participate in community volunteerism through involvement in civic groups. And the humorous things that make people laugh that you talked about are included on the list."

"And if you had to sum it all up, what would you say?" Ken asked.

Bob replied, "A fun work setting seems to be a result of a variety of things that all fit the definition of a fun work environment I gave Monika. And the other categories on the list offer some intriguing opportunities, as well. I can see that some of my employees enjoy friendly competitions, use of the exercise facilities at the local YMCA to blow off steam, other opportunities for personal development, and the occasional entertainment opportunities that were available. I can see that these categories only opened the door to a variety of other ideas that I can explore."

"Excellent," Ken said. "And how does all this fit with what you learned from Ed and Juanita?"

"Ed and Juanita have found practical ways to implement this list in each of their workplaces. But they've tailored it to fit their environment and their people."

"So what else can you apply to your situation?" Ken asked.

Bob thought for a minute and then said, "The SHRM study seems to split the ideas into two groups of activities based on popularity. The first category included items that were used by more than 80 percent of the respondents. The most popular activities were casual dress days, employee recognition and reward programs, and events where the company provided food and refreshments.

"The second group, used by 20 to 50 percent of the reporting HR managers, included a wide array of interesting approaches that contributes to a fun work environment. These include having costume dress-up days, using funny props to liven up the work environment, and creating special fun committees or 'joy gangs.' Also in this group are less obvious items such as 'bring your child to work' days, employee release time for community projects, and exercise rooms."

"So there are three activities that seem to be foundational, yet a host of ways to vary the 'fun-at-work' theme based on the individual work groups," said Ken.

"Yes," Bob said. "There is not widespread consensus as to what works best. But the majority of the items mentioned were some way of celebrating a personal achievement or having a unique and fun social event.

"And many of them include a focus on food," Ken said.

"Exactly right," Bob said. "Company picnics, chili cook-offs, Friday noon buffets, anniversary dinners, joint donut breaks, and old-fashioned ice cream socials. But also, 'food reduction' activities were also mentioned frequently under a variety of different names such as Weight Watchers, weight-reduction clubs, and Jack Sprat. Many of these ideas still follow the old tradition of breaking bread together that has long been a way to celebrate important occasions and strengthen relationships."

"So, how do you put all of this together for Monika?" Ken asked.

"I think it starts with the definition of a fun work environment I gave her in my first meeting. I think that is the guide. And, when I think of all the data I've gathered, it gives me another insight for my whiteboard:

INSIGHT #5: Strong evidence is emerging that fun workplaces can and do produce a wide array of positive physiological and psychological outcomes.

The Fear That Fun Will Be Overdone

Can you build in safeguards and specify the criteria?

"When people work as long and as hard as they do in today's competitive firms, only one thing keeps the energy flowing—fun in the workplace."

— *Don Harvey and Donald Brown*

"Find the joy in your life. Nothing else is important. Find the joy in your life."

— *The Bucket List*

"Our gift of humor is what energizes us, creates bonds, and serves as the language of our universal human experience."

— *David W. Johnson*

"Good morning, Bob. Back again, I see," Monika said as Bob knocked on her door first thing Wednesday morning. "Have a seat. Are you ready to give up this notion of creating a fun work environment yet?"

As he sat, Bob responded, "No, I'm not. Actually, my enthusiasm has grown as I've learned more about the research that exists. From what I've found, I am now convinced that having fun at work benefits both the individual and the organization. Let me tell you more."

Bob spent the next several minutes summarizing what he had heard from Ken and

what he had read in the SHRM study. Both the medical and practitioner data looked strong enough, he concluded, to investigate this further. He then went on to tell her what other successful leaders and management experts said on the subject.

"One of the books I read, *The Control Theory Manager*, included a hierarchy of needs created by psychologist William Glasser. This hierarchy starts out somewhat the same as the ones you've seen in college, but Glasser then proposes an all-powerful employee need at the top of his hierarchy—the drive to have fun, play, and engage in laughter. He suggests that this, too, is a genetic need, and that the major incentive for humans to learn is to have fun in the process. Further, he suggests that managers should combine learning and laughter into the process of teaching workers how to improve what they do. To the degree that they do this, more quality will be attained. When we laugh, when we play, when we relax, and when we enjoy ourselves in the company of mutual friends, this creates a sense of fun at work. Many other authors I've read agree with this idea.

"Glasser suggests that the need to have fun at work will often be a predominant and driving force in employees' lives. The opportunity to engage in workplace fun provides an opportunity for workers to have an all-important sense of control over some segment of their work lives, which satisfies lower needs for power and freedom, as well. Unfortunately, according to Glasser, this highest-level need for fun is often unsatisfied at work, forcing many employees to obtain their fun elsewhere. Stephen Lundin, co-author of *FiSH!*, says, 'Most workplaces are toxic energy dumps, places that are just so dead, you wonder how people could drag themselves back there every day.' Glasser even contends that many employees have learned to view the workplace as incompatible with fun, since some highly controlling managers frown upon even the appearance of fun at work. So, if you buy into Glasser's theory, which I do, a primary responsibility of all managers is to provide opportunities for employees to have fun at work. And I want to fulfill my responsibilities to my team.

"The common denominator for a fun work environment is a combination of activities that uniquely fits the people and organization, and tangibly and publicly shows an organization's concern for the person, corroborates that person's achievements and worth, creates a lighter work environment where laughter is encouraged, and stimulates the desire to make each person believe the organization is a good place to be because it makes important contributions to the community. Perhaps the impact of these fun activities is to create a corporate culture that shows a sense of appreciation of and respect for the employee and that will allow each person to conclude that this organization really is a fun place to work.

"A fun work environment contributes in key ways to job satisfaction, but only if other parts of our jobs are not negative. True job satisfaction can best result from the combination of a terrific job content and a terrific job context. I know from my college days that what makes a job satisfying is the result of some well-known factors such as autonomy, challenge, and variety. But what makes a workplace fun is less understood. Here, it seems we are capturing all the cues that managers send to tell employees they are valued, they do critical work that makes a difference, and the organization creates real value for its community. By engaging in a variety of celebratory acts, managers of fun work environments create a sense of real joy, happiness, and a positive feeling that reflects the sense of having fun at work."

"Okay," said Monika slowly as she digested what Bob had shared. "You raise some good points. Even though I am still not totally convinced, I'll let you experiment with the idea. Put together a plan for implementing it with your team along with a process for gathering some internal evidence that it does or does not work here, and a method for establishing proof before you start so we'll both know if and when you have achieved success. After six months, we'll review what your team did, look at the data, and see if you're onto something or not. Is that a fair deal?"

Bob looked at Monika gratefully. He was elated. "Yes!" he said. "My belief in the benefits of doing this is so strong that I am willing to put my reputation as a manager on the line to see if we can make it work for my team. I'll develop a plan for creating a fun work setting in my department, and a process for measuring whether or not it makes any difference to my employees or the company, as well as a method for proving the experiment's success. But I'll stick my neck out and issue an invitation to you right now to join us in the celebration."

"Okay," Monika said, "go for it, Bob, and good luck to you and your crew. Let me know what you need, and, as long as it's not too outrageous, I'll support it."

"Well," Bob said, "as long as you're volunteering, can I ask about your willingness to do a few things to help me?"

"What do you have in mind?" Monika asked.

Bob knew Monika's endorsement and formal recognition of his "fun-at-work" experiment would help get his team on board. He had thought about ways he could get Monika to send a signal to the employees about how important she thought having fun at work was. And a reward for employees who helped make the workplace fun would really get their attention.

Bob responded, "I'd like your help in doing two things. First, can I hire a local actor to come to my department and read a proclamation from you that supports the creation of a fun work setting? I know a community college student who would love the part, and his fee would be reasonable. Second, would you be willing to reinforce how serious you are about having a fun work environment here by including employee contributions to creating it as part of their annual evaluation?"

Bob knew annual evaluations got everyone's attention, so he figured adding criteria about creating a fun work environment would send a loud message as to how serious the organization was about having fun. That phrase even sounded odd to him as he reflected on it: "getting serious about having fun."

Monika responded, "Adding this to our evaluation system seems a bit extreme at this point. I'll let you hire the actor to read the proclamation, but I need some serious proof that this is a good idea before I'll go to HR and ask them to do anything to our performance-appraisal system. I'll put a little extra money in your budget as evidence of my support, but that's as far as I'm willing to go until you show me some results."

Bob left Monika's office and called Ken. "Now what do I do?" he asked. "I've got Monika's tentative support, but I also see that I am really under the gun here."

"First, congratulations," Ken said. "You've come a long way, and you've gotten permission to do something you really believe will work, right?"

"You're right," Bob said. "And thank you."

"Now for a plan!"

Over the next hour, with Ken's input, Bob decided that his plan would have three steps. Step one was to develop criteria for what types of activities would be acceptable to his team. He would have a team meeting to come up with some fun ideas, but he'd better offer some guidelines first as to what would be permissible fun and what would not be acceptable. After reflecting on what he had learned from his visits to Ed and Juanita, he revisited the definition of a fun work environment he had developed for Monika. The result was a set of guidelines he felt would work.

FIGURE 6-1

Guiding Criteria for Creating Fun Workplace Activities

Fun activities should:

1. make people smile (at a minimum) and laugh (if at all possible);
2. positively and publicly remind people of their value to the organization and to each other;
3. be inexpensive to develop, easily prepared, and implementable within time and space limitations;
4. uplift people's spirits in ways that make them feel good about being part of this organization (e.g., not embarrass, belittle, or offend anyone in or outside of the organization);
5. be as inclusive as possible while respecting the right of anyone to opt out without censure, ridicule, pressure or criticism;
6. not detract from anyone's ability to safely, professionally, or efficiently perform his or her job responsibilities;
7. contribute to, and support, the organization's culture and core values;
8. be done on a frequent basis, encompassing both planned and spontaneous events;
9. be participatively planned and implemented (not a top-down program);
10. produce organizational results that are desirable, identifiable, and measurable.

Step two would be to help his team come up with specific activities that would create a fun work setting in his department. Bob and Ken talked about what he might have to do or say to get them to buy into the idea of having fun at work. Bob decided that maybe he should touch on that point in his planning, too. After all, these employees hadn't thought about having fun at work like he had, and they weren't expecting it. This would be a real change for them, and it seemed likely that at least one person would object to this whole idea or feel it was a real waste of time. Bob agreed that he would have to think about that possibility, as well.

Step three of Bob's plan was to design the process for gathering internal evidence to prove to Monika that whatever he did had worked.

"Thanks for your help and support, Ken," Bob said. "I think I can develop a questionnaire to assess employee perceptions of the current levels and desired levels of a variety of formal and informal fun activities [Appendix 1]. I can use it both before and after the implementation of fun work activities. Using this as a measure will help me give Monika some of the proof she is looking for. It will establish whether or not there was a perceived need for fun at our company."

Ken agreed that Bob was on track to create the fun work environment he sought for himself and his employees. Bob agreed, but said, "I'm also a realist. I know that the hardest part is getting the team to buy in first. My team has to see that having a fun work environment is important and worth doing. Some people may not approve of having fun at work regardless of how it is defined.

"There are many reasons people and organizations act as if it is inappropriate to have fun in the workplace. The old notion that work is work and should not, by definition, be fun lives on in many corporations. I need to address these barriers up-front with my team to get them out in the open where they can be discussed and hopefully resolved."

"And what do you think the barriers are?" Ken asked.

Bob then listed the ones he could think of:

FIGURE 6-2
Barriers to Fun Work Environments

1. Fear of appearing inconsistent with the work culture

2. Fear that the department will look unprofessional and lose support from higher executives

3. Possible financial and productivity costs

4. No evidence that it works or contributes to personal or organizational goals

5. Fear of distracting employees from their jobs

6. Fear of looking silly

7. No time, energy, or incentives to have fun

8. Belief that "It is not part of my job."

"These inhibiting factors generally center on perceived costs, apathy, and the possible negative impact on perceptions of professionalism."

"You're right-on in seeing that any plan for creating a fun work environment has to address these barriers," Ken said "But, I'm also convinced that you see fun as

important to being productive, and you will find ways to overcome these barriers and emphasize the positive benefits of having a fun work environment. You've got a great plan; I'm sure you'll have a great kick-off meeting."

"Thanks," Bob replied.

Bob thought he was ready to kick this off, so he called a team meeting for the next Monday morning.

After everyone was assembled on Monday, he began his presentation. "I have become convinced that we need to have more fun here doing what we do. For example, I've learned that the average child laughs about five hundred times a day, while the average adult laughs only about twenty times a day. And, worse yet, as I listen to our conversations around here, I'm not sure I ever hear any laughter! This suggests that we could and should laugh more often.

"I realize there are frustrations and things that annoy us all, but we have much to celebrate and laugh about, too. Starting today, I propose that we try to find ways to have fun at work, and Monika supports this."

Just then, an actor dressed in Elizabethan attire paraded confidently in the door. After briefly bugling his presence, he unrolled a scroll, and announced a proclamation from Monika: "Henceforth, Bob's department will be a fun place to work. Everyone in this department will have fun or suffer the pain and punishment of unhappiness. Henceforth, every person who hears this proclamation is charged with the responsibility of promoting the general welfare, happiness, and pursuit of laughter. All expressions of grumpiness and grouchiness are hereby banned from this land."

The actor blew the bugle again and left the room, which was filled with both stunned and amused employees. Bob waited a few seconds for the message to sink in before continuing to speak.

"I've been reading up on this and talking to people who tell me they have fun where they work, and, quite frankly, I am envious of them. After learning about how much fun they're having and listening to you tell me what it's like working here, I've concluded three things. First, we need to have more fun here. I've not only been listening to all of you all tell me that you aren't having much fun, but I also found a study by the Work and Family Institute that shows we're not unique. That study reported that 76 percent of Generation Xers want a job that is fun. Everyone, including these young workers, wants to work in a place that's fun.

"Secondly, when I went to the bookstore and skimmed through several books by successful leaders and some management gurus, I learned that they all agree that there is a need for employees to have fun at work and that fun is important.

"The third thing I learned came from talking to a couple of respected experts: a medical doctor, Dr. Ken Berry, and our very own HR director, Madysen. Ken told me that research supports the therapeutic value of laughing on our physiology and our psychology. To paraphrase him, a laugh a day helps keeps the stress-related medical bills away.

"Madysen showed me a recent study by an HR organization that surveyed its members and discovered the reasons for and value of having fun at work. A strong majority of this HR group thought that the level of fun their employees were having at work was less than what it ought to be. By and large, they agree with what I've discovered: very few people are having the fun they should be having at work.

"The bottom line is, I'm not having fun, and I know you aren't either. Simply put, I believe that we should.

"I'm going to hand out to each of you two surveys called Perceptions of Your Fun Work Environment [Appendix 1, questions 1a-9a] and Assessing Your Overall Fun Work Environment Level [Appendix 2] to get some initial feedback from you that will help give us a foundation on which to build. You can return it to Madysen in HR by Wednesday afternoon. These surveys will help us figure out what we should do about this lack of fun.

"The HR study I mentioned also gives us a few ideas to start with. These managers provided a lengthy list of things they believe would lead to a fun work environment. The three main types of activities relate to public celebrations of professional achievements, recognition of personal milestones, and fun social events.

"Summarizing what I've learned about how to create a fun work environment, I think there are many different ways to accomplish this. For example, we could allow people to get engaged in community work projects, and I've even learned that exercise programs can help to create a fun work environment. A useful and widely held definition of a fun work environment is one in which a variety of formal and informal activities regularly occur that are designed to positively and publicly remind people of their value to their managers, their organization, and to each other through the use of humor, playful games, joyful celebrations, opportunities for self-development, or recognition of achievements and milestones. I suggest that we work together to try to create that type of fun work environment right here.

"I am convinced we need to do something different here and I want to start today," Bob said as he looked around the room at a number of stunned faces.. "We need to celebrate what we do and how we do it and what we add to our community. We need to smile and laugh more. Starting today, I'm sharing what I know about a variety of fun-related activities for you all to look at and use for our starting point. Think about how any or all of these might work for us and who we are. I can't do this by myself. You have to help me identify the actions and activities that will allow us to create a fun work setting. I have developed a set of guidelines [Figure 6-1] that I will share with you. I think they will help us get going.

"I'm also going to start off by doing a few things that I thought worked well in organizations that are like us in what they do. It will give you an idea of what I'm talking about, but keep in mind one of the important guidelines is that you need to help develop the specific things we do here or the whole notion of building a fun work setting falls on its face. Take a look at this list," Bob said as he handed out the list he'd gotten from the SHRM study with 100 Illustrations of Specific Fun-at-Work Activities [Appendix 4]. "See if it spurs any ideas you think might be a good fit for us. The list is pretty broad, so it should be a terrific starting point for us."

Janelle spoke up. "You've certainly sprung a big one on us this time," she said. "There is a lot here for us to digest."

"I know," Bob agreed, "but I think it will be pretty easy if we all agree that having a fun work environment is important. If we don't all agree, it won't happen. We must all work together to find activities that fit our team and organization, and it will add value to our lives and our company."

After the meeting, Bob returned to his office. As the afternoon progressed, he caught a couple of comments in the hall from his team. He overheard one member saying, "This is a bunch of management gobbledygook." "Sounds like one more management program du jour," said another. "Ah, but let's give it a chance," said another. Bob thought about the skepticism he was hearing and realized he had a lot of work to do to convince his own team. No one likes to see change, as it always seems to threaten what they now have, but he felt good about where he was in the change process. He had started the process of unfreezing old attitudes and maybe, if he did this right, he could make his department a model for others. He added another insight to the growing list on his whiteboard:

INSIGHT #6: You should outline guiding criteria in advance for what fun activities should aim to achieve.

Spreading the Joy

Why not let everyone help create fun?

"It has to be good. It has to be fun. It has to be profitable. When it stops being fun, do something else."

—*Dennis Benson*

"(S)he who laughs, lasts."

—*Mary Pettibone Poole*

"(In the spirit of Hamlet) I have found that to enjoy or not to enjoy, to play or not to play, to have fun or not to have fun, ahhhhhhhhhhhh, that is the question!"

—*Louis Schmier*

Bob was sold on the merits of providing his employees with the opportunity to have a fun work environment. Right after his kick-off meeting, he had hung a banner on the wall that looked like the annual United Way fund-raising thermometer, except it was labeled "Smiles per Square Foot." He had initiated, as promised, a few activities that his research told him would help create a fun work setting, and he was cautiously pleased with the response from his team so far.

In the weeks and months that followed, his team continued to buy into the "fun-at-work" idea. Periodically, he met with Ken for coffee, but now it was more often to celebrate what was happening than to get advice.

He shared with special satisfaction the enthusiasm that one of his "lunch with the team" activities had generated. Bob had asked each team member to brainstorm a handful of ideas for vanity license plates that in some way related to the theme of fun or play. His employees had jumped at the opportunity, and the collective product of their efforts produced a rather remarkable list. Some of the team members had even vowed to order their own vehicle's license plate using one of the ideas generated. More importantly, they had all gone back to their work sites and vowed to apply their reawakened creativity to their jobs!

Vanity License Plate Fun

AFUNJOB	AHAHAHA	BEHAPPY
CELEBR8	CHEERS	CHEERUP
CHERFUL	CRE8FUN	CRE8JOY
DELIGHT	DROFFUN	ECSTASY
ENJOYLF	FNATWRK	FUN4US
FUN4YOU	FUNFLOW	FUNRUS
FUNTIME	GAMES4U	GLAD4U
GOODPLA	HAPYGAL	HAPYGUY
HAVEFUN	HIGHJOY	HLAREUS
ILUVFUN	ILUVJOB	IMJOLLY
JOKETYM	JOLLITY	JOY2YOU
JOY4YOU	JOYFUL	LAFADAY
LAFALOT	LAFATWK	LAFFTER
LIFISFN	LITENUP	LUV2LAF
LUVAJOB	LUVMYCO	LUVWORK
MRHUMOR	MUCHFUN	MYJOKER
NJYMYWK	PLAALOT	PLATIME
PLAYFUL	PLAYFUL	PLAYING
PLAYTYM	PLAYWME	RESPECT
SMILE4U	VALUFUN	WKPLCFUN

On another occasion, as a conversation starter and communication exercise, Bob challenged the group to search out idiotic statements on consumer products during the next week. Coffee hour was abuzz for the next several days, as employees exchanged their discoveries with each other. Even Bob had to laugh out loud when they reported what they had found. Sample items included "Fits one head" on a shower cap, "You could be a winner! No purchase necessary. Details inside." on a bag of chips, "Do not drive car or operate machinery" on children's cough medicine; "Use like regular soap" on a bar of regular soap, "Product will be hot after heating" on frozen vegetables; "For indoor or outdoor use only" on a string of Christmas lights, "Serving suggestion: defrost" on a frozen TV dinner, "Do not turn upside down" on the bottom of a dessert box, "Guaranteed for life" on a casket in a funeral home, and, Bob's favorite, "Do not attempt to stop chain with your hands" on a chainsaw's instruction manual. All team members agreed to continue their search for additional useless phrases long after the official target date was past, due to their enjoyment of the humor generated by these items.

"These are great," Ken said. "You're well on your way to showing Monika that 'fun at work' works!"

"Yes, but I also see now that I have to get other people sharing the leadership for these activities. It can't simply be my show. I've primed the pump, but I've got to let others take the lead, as well."

"That's good thinking," Ken said. "What do you have in mind?"

"As much as I'm concerned about my time commitment, I'm even more concerned about letting others on the team create fun experiences based on their own interest and needs," Bob explained.

"Some of the books I've been reading advocate the creation of high-involvement work environments. I already allow key, competent employees to contribute their own extensive creativity to the solution of operating problems. They experience a true feeling of involvement in decision-making, they take greater pride of ownership in the decisions made, and this motivates them to follow through on the decisions to ensure their success. High involvement improves both the quality of decisions and employee commitment to them. In addition, I've seen it provide substantial gains in employee satisfaction, resulting in gains for both the department and the individual. I think I can use the same process by instituting a discussion with my team to identify things they think would be fun to do and would create a fun work environment."

"I agree with you," Ken said. "Let me know how it goes."

Several days later, Bob launched this next phase of "fun at work." He scheduled a lunch with his team built around the theme "launching a fun space" mission. Before the lunch, Bob asked each team member to think up one good idea that he or she had for making the department a fun place to work and bring it to the lunch. The rules were simple. First, each person had to develop one suggestion, whether it was initially seen as practical or not. Second, the ideas could be derived from the list he'd handed out from SHRM, but should at least be adapted or modified in some way. The goal was to suggest something that would work in this department with these employees. Bob figured this was one way to overcome some of the resistance he had heard about, since everyone would have to come up with something regardless of its creativity. Bob knew that getting people to verbalize an idea publicly was one way to win them over. He knew the range of activities on the list he handed out was so diverse that even the biggest critic in his department could find something to love.

At the lunch meeting, Bob found he was right, but it took a bit of cajoling. He had been warned that one of the senior engineers, Kjell, was particularly outspoken in his criticism of this idea of having fun at work. So Bob started with Kjell.

"Say, Kjell," Bob asked, "what did you come up with as an idea for creating a fun work environment here?"

Kjell responded, "Well, I really think this fun stuff is rather hokey. I don't know what ideas I have that could improve on what I have now. I'm pretty happy with things the way they are."

Bob responded, "Terrific. I am delighted that you're happy. But tell me, Kjell, why are you happy, and isn't there anything we could do differently around here to make you happier about coming to work?"

Kjell said, "I love my job and this company. They gave me a job when I really needed one and stood by me when I had some medical problems a few years ago. I'm happy every day I come to work."

Bob thought a moment and said, "That's great that you are happy about working here. In fact, I am going to give you the unofficial title of Corporate Cheerleader. But are you having fun, too? After all, being happy and having fun seem to me to be two related but different things."

"I agree," Kjell responded, "but I don't know if it's right to have fun when you're working. It just doesn't seem appropriate for some reason. But I am willing to be called the Corporate Cheerleader, as I certainly am that."

Bob said, "Look at the list, Kjell. Is there anything there that we can all do to make this feel like a fun place to work—for others, as well as for yourself?"

Kjell scanned the list and finally said, "Well, I'm not certain I still agree with all this, but there are some ideas I like. Participating in community activities or getting professional and personal recognition isn't something that makes anyone laugh necessarily, but it sure does make a difference when we get these indications of respect and appreciation or have a chance to represent the company to outsiders. How about writing down my suggestion of a company-paid formal dinner whenever anyone receives his or her PE designation? I think that would be great."

"Good idea," Bob said. "How about you, Janelle? What ideas do you have?"

"Well," Janelle said, "I'm the one who told you that you had dumped on us when you presented all this stuff, but I'll tell you what: I like the idea of having more fun anywhere and especially here. Since you're handing out titles, how about designating me as the Goddess of Fun?"

Bob laughed, "That works for me, and I don't think any of the rest of us really seek that title anyway. Wear it with pride."

"Now that that's settled," Janelle continued, "let me contribute my idea for the team's consideration. I like that the power company simulates problems with its nuclear reactor to keep the staff in fighting form. How about if we invent something like that here? If we all came up with five technical questions about our field of environmental engineering, we could set aside a time once a week to play our own version of Trivial Pursuit. We could have a Casey Jones Award and give the victor an engineer's hat to wear or display on his or her desk during the time between contests. We'd need to make up some rules to keep it fair as we are all working on different projects, but I think this would be a blast, plus it would keep us sharp and up to date on what's going on in our field. What do you think of that idea?"

"A great one to add to our unique list of what we can do to make this a fun workplace," Bob said. "Who's next?"

"Let me take a whack at this," Thao said. "First," she added, "I will henceforth be known as the Funmeister. I'm an old Saturday Night Live fan, and this title is at last mine. Now as far as my idea, I like the idea of getting two-fers out of this. After all, aren't we supposed to be finding ways to make the work fun while also improving our productive efforts? My idea, then, is to use our customer letters to both lighten up what we do, and also learn from our customers at the same time. Let me give you an example that no one has seen, since management never shows customer complaint letters to anyone but the person who is affected. I think it's so funny that I don't mind sharing with you." Thao then unfolded a photocopy and began reading:

Dear Apex Environmental Engineering Company:

Last week, I called your company seeking its expertise on an environmental problem my organization has. We produce health food and specialize in garlic and garlic-related products. We strive to hire people who actively share our philosophy about the health benefits of using our product, and we have been very successful with about two-thirds of our workforce being committed to using our products on a regular basis. Many of them are also vegans or vegetarians and don't believe in using products that have artificial ingredients in them. Our problem is that the other one-third of our employees find the working environment somewhat odious. We are receiving a number of complaints and threats of unionization, and we are suffering extremely high turnover.

    We were referred to Ms. Thao Meister for her response. ["Now you know why I wanted to be called the Funmeister," Thao interjected.] *We found her laughter as we described the problem to be irritating and her suggestion as to how to correct it ("Give your employees deodorant.") to be offensive. We think we have a serious problem and were hoping that your organization could help us. The reaction of Ms. Meister was so intolerable that we will never seek to do business with you again and hope that you find an appropriate way to discipline her.*

Sincerely,

Paul Swenson
President, OGP

Thao finished reading the letter and looked up to see everyone smiling broadly.

"You see what I mean?" said Thao. "I know I shouldn't have laughed and that these folks were serious about their problem, but think of how this would hit you first thing in the morning. This was just too hilarious not to laugh. I have been properly reprimanded for my response to it, and I fully understand why.

"My point is that everyone messes up like this now and then, and we could take the funnier letters and use them to talk about customer service and how to see things through our clients' eyes. If nothing else, it would give us a laugh while reminding us of the many funny things customers do and how seriously we need to treat them. I remember hearing the old Walt Disney story about how many guests ask the Disney employees, 'What time is the three o'clock parade?' We all get crazy questions, and they make us laugh, but they also have a serious purpose that is worth talking about. I think that would be fun."

"Well," Bob said, still chuckling, "we're about to run out of time today, but does anyone have one more to share before we get back to work?"

"How about me?" Ruth Lillian asked. "I'd like to be called the Minister of Fun."

Bob thought, *Will wonders never cease?* as he had always thought of Ruth Lillian as a very serious woman. "Go ahead," he said, "let's hear your idea."

"Well," Ruth Lillian said, "I like to do puzzles, and I especially like to do those puzzles where you have to figure out what the word or phrase is by looking at a simple drawing like you see in the comic sections of the Sunday papers. I think some people call them Wuzzles.

"For example, if I drew a picture that had the word 'reading' and a line above and below it, the puzzle answer would be 'reading between the lines.' I sketched out a few while you were coming up with other ideas, and I'd like to show you what I am talking about. My idea is to have a contest that asks each of us to create one of these on a monthly basis. Then the person who creates the most creative puzzle that month wins a prize of some kind. All the puzzles would have to be related to our business in some way, so, like Janelle's idea, we could also benefit from being reminded about something important that we do while having some fun with the puzzles."

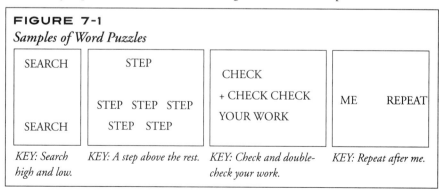

FIGURE 7-1
Samples of Word Puzzles

SEARCH SEARCH	STEP STEP STEP STEP STEP STEP	CHECK + CHECK CHECK YOUR WORK	ME REPEAT
KEY: Search high and low.	KEY: A step above the rest.	KEY: Check and double-check your work.	KEY: Repeat after me.

"Wow," Bob said. "I really like these ideas. I think that we are off to a good start in coming up with some ways to help bump my smile barometer up a notch or two. I can hardly wait to talk about these further. Before we meet next time, if you didn't already, I'd like to have the rest of you think up some other ideas for us to discuss. After everyone has a turn, we will discuss them and decide which ones make sense for us to try, okay? I hope everyone has a great day, and I'll see you at our next 'launching a fun space' meeting."

Several weeks went by, and everyone had a turn during one of the luncheons. Now it was time to move forward. At Friday's weekly staff meeting, Bob got the normal agenda issues out of the way and then reserved the last ten minutes for a discussion of an item tantalizingly called "Spreading the Fun." When he got to this point, he could see several people sit up a little straighter, and everyone had inquisitive looks on their faces. He paused just a moment to crank up the suspense one notch further before beginning.

"We've gotten off to a good start, I think, on my goal of building a fun work environment," Bob said. "My lunchtime conversations with you indicate you feel the same way, have some great ideas as to how to create a fun work environment, and want this process to continue. Here is what I propose. Let's set up a schedule whereby each of you agrees to take primary responsibility for planning and initiating one or more fun ideas during one month of the year. What do you think?" he asked hopefully.

There was a momentary pause that caused Bob's heart to race a little faster. Then, with smiles breaking out on everyone's faces, people stepped up to the plate. "I'll do it," Margrete said. "Me, too," Praveen said. "I'd like to go first, as I've already got several ideas," Daunte offered. One by one, they all signed on for one of the months in the coming year starting with January. Bob was elated.

"What's our reward for doing this extra task?" asked one of his staff playfully. Before Bob could respond with his highly expected, "I don't have any more money in the budget," Margrete piped up with an idea. "I think we should at least be given the opportunity to create a fun new title for ourselves that captures the essence of our new responsibility." "That's a great suggestion," added Praveen. "And let's make them as wild and descriptive as they can be."

"Fine with me," said Bob. "Let's make the monthly assignments right now [Figure 7-2] and attach titles to each of you for that month."

FIGURE 7-2

Humorous Job Titles and Monthly Fun Responsibilities

Month	Person	Title
January	Kjell	Corporate Cheerleader
February	Margrete	Jollytologist
March	Praveen	Funcilitator
April	Janelle	Goddess of Fun
May	Maili	Chief Fun Manager
June	Rajiv	Fun R Us Team Leader
July	Daunte	Joy Team Captain
August	Tawanna	Glee Club Leader
September	Ruth Lillian	Minister of Fun
October	Anne-Marie	No. 1 Funologist
November	Hunter	Director of Fun
December	Thao	Funmeister

"As the overall coordinator, how about if I take the title of Fun Minute Manager to help out where and when I can?" Bob said to his staff. All heads nodded a vigorous endorsement.

A few days went by, and Bob overheard a lot of excited talk about the major events his staff was already planning. Each staff member seemed to be determined to outdo every other person. *Uh-oh,* he thought, *this process may have gotten out of hand already. I've got to keep this under control.*

When Friday's staff meeting came around and the critical items were resolved, Bob directed the group's attention to the issue of fun again. "Before we go off in our own directions," he said, "I think you'll all agree that we should review our guidelines again. After all, we must recognize that anything we do in our department will be scrutinized by everyone else; we'll be under a microscope all year long." Several heads

nodded in reluctant agreement. "Please pull out the guideline sheet I gave you, and scan through it to see how we're doing."

There was some thoughtful silence until Janelle spoke up.

"Gee, Bob," she said, "you must have been paying close attention to what your friends told you about creating a fun work setting, because I can't see much to add to what we talked about earlier."

"I agree," Ruth Lillian said, "I think we have some really good criteria."

"Okay," Bob said, "let me remind you of just a couple that we need to make sure we pay close attention to. Remember, the idea is not to make fun of your co-workers or of management. In addition, we must be careful to avoid telling harmful or risky jokes—the ones that make fun of an ethnic group or put down a class of human beings or involve unacceptable language. We should also be careful to avoid being overly sarcastic, or playing disruptive practical jokes or pranks on others that they might not appreciate. Can we all agree to that?" Bob noted that all heads nodded in grateful agreement; no one wanted feelings intentionally hurt.

"Anything else?" Bob asked, as the room slowly got quieter.

"There's one more that I'd like to stress again," Anne-Marie offered. "You're already demonstrating it by the way you conducted the meetings. I think humor and joy and fun are best inserted into the workplace on a participative basis, and not imposed from above." Again, heads nodded their affirmation.

"Okay," Bob said. "The last thing I want to stress today is that we're not in competition with each other. Some of our attempts at fun will succeed brilliantly, and others may bomb miserably. That's okay. But we don't want to get consumed by all of this planning of fun activities, either. Remember that Guideline #8 suggests that many of these activities are best done on a spontaneous basis.

"Anyway, I'll put the guidelines on the bulletin board where we can all refer back to them as we plan our events each month. Then, at the end of the year, we can use the criteria to evaluate ourselves to see how closely we stuck to them." A few days later, he posted the Guiding Criteria for Creating Fun Workplace Activities, for all of his employees to refer to on a regular basis.

Bob sat back in his office chair and reflected on the progress to date. He was pleased to note that he had stumbled onto another insight that he could add to his emerging list; this one built on the solid benefits of a participative approach. In thinking about the products of a high-involvement approach to fun at work, however, he realized that

it was crucial not to force anyone to engage in an activity he or she felt uncomfortable with. As a result, he added four bullet points to the insight that reflected the idea of tailoring the fun activities to fit the interest level of those employees involved:

INSIGHT #7: Using the principles of a high-involvement workplace, consultation with employees can provide a strong base of support and innumerable ideas for fun at work.

- If it's fun for all, then have a ball.

- If it's fun for a few, then follow through (with only them).

- If it's fun for just one, let him or her take it and run (alone).

- If it's fun for none, then leave it undone.

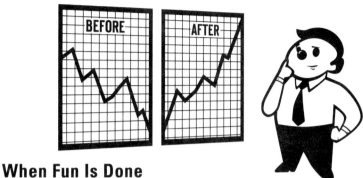

When Fun Is Done

Can you measure the results?

"You don't work for a dollar—you work to create and have fun."
—*Walt Disney*

"Companies which champion fun have higher productivity and profitability."
—*Bill Capodagli and Lynn Jackson*

"There are four major shared values at AES: to act with integrity, to be fair, to have fun, and to be socially responsible."
—*Dennis Bakke*

Six months into his experiment, Bob was preparing to bring the results of his "fun-at-work" environment to Monika. News of Bob's success in creating a fun workplace within and by his group of employees had spread like wildfire. Managerial colleagues were constantly stopping him in hallways, after meetings, and during coffee breaks to ask him what was going on in his department.

"What are these crazy job titles for each employee I keep hearing about?" asked one.

"What's with that 'Smile Barometer' I see posted in your department each week?" asked another.

"Man, the 'Happiness Quotient' must be at an all-time high among your employees!" exclaimed a third.

"I wish my department had as many 'Smiles per Square Foot' as your department does," interjected a fourth peer.

"Whatever you put into their water to keep them happy must be contagious, since it sure seems to have spread throughout your whole unit and down into the lower ranks, too," suggested yet another.

Bob smiled broadly in response to each of these comments, but he knew that part of his annual review by Monika would include how well his experiment had worked. *When you put your neck on the line,* Bob thought, *the potential feeling of exhilaration is matched only by a deep fear that you might also be wrong.* Bob knew it was time to find out. How to prove to Monika that having fun at work was worth it was a real challenge. While he could feel that things were vastly improved when he walked into his unit's area or talked with his staff, he knew he couldn't just convince Monika by reporting his good feeling, or even the positive comments from his colleagues. Proving that this was worth the time and trouble it took was top priority on Bob's list of things to do.

Well, Bob thought, *for starters, I should use the same tests I used when we began to follow through on my process for gaining internal evidence.* So Bob dug out the two questionnaires he had used at the beginning of the experiment in order to administer them again. He went to Madysen and asked her to administer the questionnaires to his team so he wouldn't influence the results. She readily agreed to do so.

Two weeks later, the results were tabulated and returned to him. Overall, things looked great. The first questionnaire, Perceptions of Your Fun Work Environment, addressed the degree to which the ten categories of fun activities were used, both before and after the experiment. Most of the mean scores, on a scale of 1 to 5, had jumped from between 1 and 2 to around 4. This clearly showed that his employees now recognized the presence of many different types of fun-related actions that had been initiated from within the team itself. *So far, so good,* Bob thought.

TABLE 8-1

Perceptions of Your Fun Work Environment

Category	Before	After
Humor	1.1	4.5
Personal growth	1.7	3.6
Public celebrations	2.3	3.8
Entertainment	1.0	3.9
Games	1.3	4.0
Social events	1.6	4.7
Recognition of milestones	1.5	4.1
Volunteer opportunities	1.6	4.2
Stress-relief activities	1.4	3.7
Friendly competitions	1.1	3.8
Overall	1.46	4.03

Next, he created a gap analysis that looked at differences between the reported current level of activities and employee perceptions of how much they thought there should be. The gaps, which had previously been as wide as possible, now showed only a few areas where the team members still wanted increased activity. Only "Personal growth" and "Stress-relief activities" showed a modest gap of 1.0 or more.

TABLE 8-2

Gap Analysis for Fun Activities

Category	Is Now	Should Be	Gap
Humor	4.5	4.8	0.3
Personal growth	3.6	4.6	1.0
Public celebrations	3.8	4.7	0.9
Entertainment	3.9	4.0	0.1
Games	4.0	4.2	0.2
Social events	4.7	4.7	0.0
Recognition of milestones	4.1	4.8	0.7
Volunteer opportunities	4.2	4.2	0.0
Stress-relief activities	3.7	4.8	1.1
Friendly competitions	3.8	4.1	0.3
Overall	4.03	4.49	0.46

Next, Bob examined the results from Assessing Your Overall Fun Work Environment Level [Appendix 2]. This one simply assessed, both before and after the experiment, employee perceptions of the overall fun work environment that they were experiencing. The individual scores, which could range between 20 and 100, showed a huge gain in the reported level of their positive work experience; the overall mean skyrocketed from near the bottom (1.35) to something substantially higher (4.20). Clearly, these data suggested that employees were now having fun. The burning question remained: Was it coming at the expense of results?

Bob then turned his attention to the results from Perceived Impact of Fun on Organizational Outcomes [Appendix 3]. This assessed his employees' perceptions of personal and organizational results on ten dimensions including attitudes, stress, productivity, respect, work outcomes (absenteeism/attendance/turnover), commitment, corporate culture, communications, work behaviors, and quality of work. Here, the results were a bit more equivocal, but still mostly positive. The overall average score was 42 on a scale ranging from a low of 10 to a high of 50. Highest results were reported in the areas of employee attitudes, work behaviors, stress relief, and respect and caring for each other. Apparently, however, employees were less certain that fun at work produced substantial gains in quality of work. Overall, Bob was pleased to note that results of all ten categories showed scores on the positive end of the scale, thereby implying a belief in the causal connection between fun at work and a variety of payoffs.

TABLE 8-3

Perceived Impact of Fun on Organizational Outcomes

Result Area	Mean Score
Employee attitudes	4.4
Stress and tension relief	4.7
Productivity	3.8
Respect and caring	4.7
Work outcomes	4.0
Employee commitment	4.1
Corporate culture	4.2
Communications	4.3
Employee work behaviors	4.4
Quality of work	3.7
Overall score:	42.3

Bob was extremely pleased with what he saw. But he was not going to rest his case entirely on the questionnaires. He went back to HR and asked Madysen for her help once again.

"Madysen," he said, "can you tell me if the job satisfaction survey that we administer each year has any relevant data that I can look at it? I'm hoping to gather several different measures that can help me convince Monika that our efforts to create a fun work environment paid off. I know the job satisfaction survey we do annually can be broken down by department. I want to see my department's results to discover if that measure captured anything else that would supplement the data from the questionnaires I developed on my own."

Madysen said, "I'll go you one better. I've been following what you've been doing because I think it is a really good idea. I was glad to see someone finally take the lead to make this a more fun place to work. I have been collecting some data of my own across the past six months to see what I could learn about how this experiment is working out. Here are some turnover results, data on the length of time to fill positions, attendance figures, customer satisfaction scores, work-related claims, and even budget data. I'll tell you right now that I'm impressed with what's happening, and you should be happy, too. The thing a lot of us look at first—your customer satisfaction scores—have gone up in comparison with the rest of the company. You should be really pleased. After all, isn't that the most important thing we measure? But the other scores have gone up, too. Your staff has higher attendance rates, lower turnover, and it is easier to recruit new employees for your team. It's amazing when we listen to new hires, because all they want to talk about is how much they found the work environment in your team to be fun. If you need me to go with you to talk to Monika, let me know because I am a real believer and a supporter."

Bob was pleased to hear all of this. He was realistic enough to know, however, that the data needed to be carefully interpreted with such a small sample, but he felt really good.

Armed with his results, Bob headed toward Monika's office the next morning.

"Well, Bob," Monika said. "Tell me about your little experiment. Did the extra dollars I gave you for buying donuts make a difference, and did the actor I hired to read that fun proclamation leave any lasting impact? By the way, I sure caught a lot of grief from my peers on that little stunt. Everyone's calling me 'Her Royal Majesty Monika of Engineering,' and my peers tell me that I'm spending money like a fool."

Bob replied, "I think I can show you the strong evidence you've been seeking. I

am very pleased to tell you my experiment is a great success. Not only do the results of my own survey show a definite improvement in creating a fun workplace, but Madysen gave me some extra ammunition from our company-wide survey results, as well. Look at this." Bob confidently showed Monika the before and after data from his employee attitude surveys.

After a few minutes of examining the data, Monika said, "Looks good! They really believe they're having more fun now, don't they? How about other performance measures? After all, these data I'm looking at represent only employee attitudes and perceptions."

Bob responded, "I think it's too early, and my sample is too small for any valid conclusions on performance improvements, but let's look at a few critical measures. For example, look at the data on attendance. Obviously you can't perform well if you aren't here on a regular basis, and my team's numbers look pretty good. Also, turnover is down, and that means I don't have to incur the costs of recruiting and training new people. Finally, customer satisfaction with my team's projects is up. Let me show you a few letters to back up the numbers I got from our marketing department on customer feedback."

Monika read a few lines of each letter. "Well done, Bob. I'm rapidly becoming convinced that you are onto something here. Your data are impressive. Maybe having fun isn't the silly idea I thought it was when you first came to me to talk about it. I've got to be honest, though. I really thought you were nuts. Maybe there is something to a fun work environment after all," Monika acknowledged.

Bob left feeling pretty good about his conversation with Monika. Sitting back in his office, he could look out at the team's work space. He saw jokes posted on the wall, one of his people had painted her work space pink, and another had his daughter sitting next to him while he explained what an environmental engineer did. He could feel the happiness and see the smiles.

Glancing up at his whiteboard, Bob saw the need to add another insight to his list. This one literally flowed from his fingertips, as he wrote:

INSIGHT #8: The only way to conclusively determine and demonstrate the actual effects attributable to fun at work is to measure and compare them on a pretest and posttest basis.

Becoming a Fun Minute Manager

What guidelines exist for implementing a Fun-at-Work program?

"I have enjoyed all the challenges we have taken at Virgin Airlines, so because I'm having fun doing what I do, the risk factor takes second place."
                    —*Richard Branson*
"We don't stop playing because we grow old; we grow old because we stop playing."
                    —*George Bernard Shaw*
"Attempt to create the most fun workplace in the history of the world."
                    —*Dennis Bakke*

A few months went by before Monika called with some unexpected news.

"Guess what?" she said. "I have you scheduled to make a presentation to our senior management team at next month's executive meeting. The word has gotten out about our experiment, and the CEO asked me to get us all some information on what you are doing and how it works. Can you do it?"

Bob thought, *Wow. This is great.*

"Yes," he said, "I'd be delighted to do this. See you next month." With a satisfied smile, Bob hung up and wondered how he could explain what he was doing to someone else. He also noticed, with hidden pleasure, Monika had started to call it "our experiment."

Bob leaned back in his chair and thought about an overall theme for his talk. Suddenly he bolted upright and moved quickly to the chalkboard. *I've got it!* he thought. He grabbed a marker and wrote his newest and most comprehensive insight at the bottom of his previous list:

INSIGHT #9: Fun-at-work programs can be designed and implemented quickly, easily, and inexpensively by a truly committed Fun Minute Manager and his or her team.

The next few weeks flew by, and soon it was time for Bob's presentation. After a strong endorsement of Bob's success by the CEO in his introductory remarks, it was time for Bob to begin.

His first words to these high-level executives were simple and pointed. "Let me start by asking you five rhetorical questions. First, how many of you think you're having enough fun doing your job? Second, how many of you think your employees at all levels of the organization are having enough fun doing their jobs? Third, do you think this would be a better place to work if we were all having fun while doing our jobs? Fourth, do you believe there would be any personal and organizational benefits if employees had more fun around here? Fifth, if the answers to the third and fourth questions are 'yes,' why in heaven's name don't we do something to create a fun work environment?"

Bob paused to let the impact of those questions and their implicit answers sink in. He could almost see the wheels spinning in the minds of these seasoned executives.

"I am a recovering 'all-work-and-no-play' manager who has seen the light. Now," Bob said, "I have redefined myself as the Fun Minute Manager in the department where I try to be a passionate model for infusing fun into the workplace, and it can be done quickly and easily. I see myself as someone whose job includes, but is not limited to, an ongoing search for ways to provide and support activities that will embellish employee feelings of self-respect, encourage employees to enjoy a bit of levity, and advance the goals of the organization.

"Now, ten months into our fun-at-work pilot, our department has seen higher attendance rates than the company average and improved customer satisfaction scores. We also have lower turnover, and recruiting for our department is easier than before.

"I believe I can show a strong correlation between these organizational benefits and our fun-at-work venture based on pretesting and posttesting we did. Let me share why we created a plan and how we implemented this process."

Bob went on to summarize how the atmosphere in his department had been rather somber at one time, with little cooperation, support, joy, or positive energy. Then, after he experienced a "fun epiphany," he made a genuine attempt to create a high-involvement work environment. Now all staff members had voluntarily taken responsibility for creating a fun workplace. He showed his PowerPoint slide with his Categories for Fun-at-Work Activities [Figure 5-1] he had shown Monika earlier. He then reviewed numerous examples of the many types of fun events that had occurred and some of those that were already scheduled for the next year. He noted from the many raised eyebrows that much of this was new territory to explore.

Bob showed them his slide on Guiding Criteria for Creating Fun Workplace Activities [Figure 6-1] and carefully noted how he and his staff had agreed in advance on the guiding criteria for each fun activity.

Glancing around the room, Bob was pleased to note that many heads were nodding in agreement with this critical step. He had, he believed, struck an important chord with them in being careful not to let the process get out of control.

Bob then drew a deep breath and took a couple of risks with this results-oriented and down-to-earth audience. "First," he said, "I recognize fully that there are some potentially valid reasons why fun at work might not succeed in some workplaces—and I wouldn't be surprised if some of you are already way ahead of me on this issue."

Bob paused for dramatic effect, noted some knowing smiles, and then continued. "It might be too substantial a change in the organization's culture for it to be accepted, or it may not receive support from higher executives like yourselves. Then there is the fear that customers, or even the employees in other departments or units, will react negatively. Someone will legitimately raise concerns about safety issues, and others will express fears that fun will prove too costly or negatively impact organizational productivity. Finally, it is possible that some employees, particularly those predisposed by cultural backgrounds, won't wish to get involved at first. They might be concerned about saving face and be afraid that the fun activities will make them look silly and embarrass them. These are all legitimate issues that we have confronted and slowly worked through to our own satisfaction.

"The final theme I'd like to touch on is really important, especially from the

standpoint of spreading this gospel of fun to other organizations. I really think I have some lessons to share regarding how to go about doing it, but first I'd like to explain conceptually how the process works," he said. "Many of you have told me repeatedly that a picture is worth a thousand words, and so I've created a practical diagram showing the flow of steps that we've taken to implement and assess the impact of a fun work environment."

Projecting Figure 9-1 on the large screen behind him, Bob proceeded to emphasize the critical importance of measuring the employees' attitudes toward the idea of having fun at work in advance; assuring compatibility of fun with the overall organizational culture; participatively embracing a fun philosophy; brainstorming multiple fun tactics and strategies; and developing criteria and guidelines that are perceived, understood, and accepted by employees.

FIGURE 9-1

Diagram of the Participative Fun at Work Process

Pre-assessment of receptivity to fun (baseline)
▼
Attainment of organizational support (managerial buy-in)
▼
Adoption of a fun-at-work philosophy and culture
▼
Recognition of possible impediments to fun at work
▼
Creation of guiding criteria for fun-at-work efforts
▼
Development of fun-oriented activities, programs, and cues
▼
Assessment of attitudinal and behavioral changes
▼
Assessment of personal and organizational results
▼
Celebration of success and recommitment to fun

Then he laid out the potential and actual positive results from a fun workplace in four domains based on his questionnaire responses:

- employee work-related attitudes (e.g., higher satisfaction, respect for others, energy/enthusiasm, organizational commitment, and lower alienation and boredom);
- employee work behaviors (e.g., increased civility, cooperation, communication, and organizational citizenship; less complaints and grievances);

- the consequences for organizational results (e.g., improved quantity and quality of productivity, increased customer satisfaction, higher ability to attract new employees; lower absenteeism, tardiness, and turnover); and

- personal benefits (e.g., stress and tension relief).

Bob again saw several heads nodding enthusiastically, and he knew his visual presentation focusing on results had resonated with them.

"Next," Bob said, "I want to tell you how excited I am to share with you these nine key insights from my journey of personal discovery [Figure 9-2]. They provide a strong foundation for the action principles or guidelines that follow for New Fun Minute Managers [Figure 9-3].

FIGURE 9-2

Summary of Insights into Fun Workplaces

INSIGHT #1: You can get a lot of people to do a lot of things, such as work on service projects, hold elective office, work longer hours, or donate money, if there is an element of fun.

INSIGHT #2: Most people want to have fun while also doing meaningful and productive work.

INSIGHT #3: A wide range of activities exist that can provide fun even in serious work environments.

INSIGHT #4: Fun at work is not historically viewed as an integral part of a manager's responsibilities. Consequently, it will not be easily accepted by superiors without compelling evidence.

INSIGHT #5: Strong evidence is emerging that fun workplaces can and do produce a wide array of positive physiological and psychological outcomes.

INSIGHT #6: You should outline guiding criteria in advance for what fun activities should aim to achieve.

INSIGHT #7: Using the principles of a high-involvement workplace, consultation with employees can provide a strong base of support and innumerable ideas for fun at work.

INSIGHT #8: The only way to conclusively determine and demonstrate the actual effects attributable to fun at work is to measure and compare them on a pretest and posttest basis.

INSIGHT #9: Fun-at-work programs can be designed and implemented quickly, easily, and inexpensively by a truly committed Fun Minute Manager and his or her team.

"Finally," Bob concluded, "I'd like to share with you my suggestions and guidelines for how you might go about implementing such a program—but only if you feel it is appropriate for you. Here are my most powerful suggestions—my own ten-step program for creating a fun workplace," Bob said as he began to display each of them on the projection screen.

FIGURE 9-3

Guidelines for New Fun Minute Managers

1. Address other employee needs first (job content).
2. Make sure that fun-at-work will be a good fit with the organization's culture and with employee expectations.
3. Build a fun workplace on an underlying philosophical foundation, not just a set of mechanical practices.
4. Make a long-term commitment to fun as an ongoing process, not a short-term program.
5. Become more playful yourself.
6. Involve others in creating fun experiences.
7. Satisfy employee needs for recognition in new and unique ways.
8. Use a wide variety of fun-related activities.
9. Capitalize on the surprise factor.
10. Assess and regularly monitor your success at creating a fun work culture.

"Let me address each of these points briefly. First, you'd better make sure that other employee needs are addressed reasonably well. To paraphrase psychologist William Glasser, fun is not a replacement for job security, adequate compensation, or even autonomy or challenge in one's job. To put it bluntly, employees won't laugh at your humor or appreciate a celebration of a birthday or enjoy a humorous skit if they are angry about shortcomings in their physical and psychological work environment. Fun should be introduced after other contemporary ingredients are in place and job content has been enriched, and not as a substitute for them.

"Second, make sure that you and your employees fully understand and agree on the current organizational culture. Identify the culture's explicit and implicit values, norms, and practices, and then decide whether they allow for and support the presence of a fun workplace. Also, check systematically with your employees to see if they want more fun at work. For example, we provided a simple questionnaire and used the collective results to guide our decisions. If not, don't try to force-fit fun into the culture.

"Third, ask yourself why you are really thinking about implementing a fun workplace. Make sure that your heart is in it. Also, and this is important, spend time understanding the conceptual foundations for fun work practices like those discussed earlier, because this will help you understand how fun produces desired results. Don't just charge in and blindly implement a borrowed set of fun workplace ideas and gimmicks. You need to be able to answer 'Why are we doing this?' if anyone asks.

"Fourth, remember many employees are inclined to reject new programs, especially if they believe you are not going to stick with them over the long haul. Therefore, you need to make a strong commitment to a fun workplace, and communicate a long-term vision of it to your employees. Don't be guilty of making a big splash at the start and then allowing the program to fizzle out a short while later.

"Fifth, look into the mirror and candidly ask yourself whether you are afflicted with terminal seriousness. Learn to laugh, learn to share humor with others, learn to watch for humor in all parts of life around you. And most critically, learn to become more playful yourself. You cannot expect others to help create a fun workplace if their primary role model is a stick-in-the-mud. This may take some effort, work, and time, but you need to make a strong personal commitment to think, plan, and personally initiate a host of fun activities.

"Sixth, don't go it alone. Take a cue from the CEOs of Ben & Jerry's, who created a 'Joy Gang' and charged it with making sure that all employees have fun. And Cold Stone Creamery took this a step further when managers asked employees to be sure that the customers have fun. Draw on the motivational effects of participation, and involve others in the creation of fun experiences at work.

"Seventh, accept the fact that most employees have a very strong need for personal recognition, and it is seldom fully satisfied at work. Remember the adage 'The sweetest sound in the entire world is the sound of our own name being called when awards are given.' Place high emphasis on satisfying employee needs for recognition by finding a multitude of ways in which to celebrate key anniversaries, wins, accomplishments, gains, and successes.

"Eighth, don't get stuck in a rut, despite the temptation to hold the same events, tell the same jokes, and pass out the same awards year after year. Tap into the creativity of yourself and others to develop a wide variety of fun-related activities. Remember 'different strokes for different folks,' and use it to develop unique approaches for each employee. You can use the examples provided by others [Appendix 4] to start your

thinking, but commit yourself to move far afield from just replicating the tactics used by others. Creativity is necessary.

"Ninth, don't allow yourself to become predictable. Instead, capitalize on the surprise factor to keep people on a positive edge of anticipation and never quite knowing what is coming next. Be unpredictable; be experimental; try different things even though they won't always produce the type of reaction you hope for.

"Last, don't guess at your own success. There will always be those who think this is all silly and unproductive. If someone who doesn't believe in having fun at work challenges you to substantiate your efforts, have some strong documentation. We survey our employees annually anyway, so this should be easy to do. Remember, we're all engineers. Nothing speaks louder than quantitative data about the results of a fun work environment, although you can certainly couple this with personal reports and anecdotes from employees, too. For those of you who are interested, I've provided sample assessment instruments for you [Appendices 1, 2, and 3]. I've also created some lists of fun activities, acknowledged fun workplaces, fun and humor websites, and books on workplace fun [Appendices 4, 5, 6, and 7].

"So, that's it," Bob concluded. "You now have my ten-step program for creating a fun workplace." As he began to acknowledge the enthusiastic applause from his senior colleagues, he removed his tie, unbuttoned his shirt, and revealed a T-shirt underneath with huge letters reading:

TAKE THIS JOB AND LOVE IT!

APPENDIX 1

Perceptions of Your Fun Work Environment

Introduction: A fun workplace culture is one in which a variety of formal and informal activities regularly occur that are designed to positively and publicly remind people of their value to their managers, the organization, and each other through the use of humor, playfulness, joyful expressions, opportunities for self satisfaction, or personal recognition.

Directions: Assess your company on the following 10 two-part measures, using the five-point response scale as shown. Circle one number for both parts of each question.

Low Degree   **High Degree**

1   2   3   4   5

1a. The amount of humor we have here now.

1   2   3   4   5

1b. The amount of humor that we should have.

1   2   3   4   5

2a. The amount of opportunities for personal growth we have here now.

1   2   3   4   5

2b. The amount of opportunities for personal growth we should have.

1   2   3   4   5

3a. The amount of public celebrations of professional achievement we have here now.

1   2   3   4   5

3b. The amount of public celebrations of professional achievements we should have.

1   2   3   4   5

4a. The amount of entertainment we have here now.

1   2   3   4   5

4b. The amount of entertainment we should have.

1   2   3   4   5

5a. The amount of games we have here now.

1	2	3	4	5

5b. The amount of games we should have.

1	2	3	4	5

6a. The amount of social events we have now.

1	2	3	4	5

6b. The amount of social events we should have.

1	2	3	4	5

7a. The amount of recognition of personal milestones we have here now.

1	2	3	4	5

7b. The amount of recognition of personal milestones we should have.

1	2	3	4	5

8a. The amount of opportunities to engage in community volunteerism we have here now.

1	2	3	4	5

8b. The amount of opportunities to engage in community volunteerism we should have.

1	2	3	4	5

9a. The amount of stress-relief activities we have here now.

1	2	3	4	5

9b. The amount of stress-relief activities we should have.

1	2	3	4	5

10a. The amount of friendly competitions we have here now.

1	2	3	4	5

10b. The amount of friendly competitions we should have.

1	2	3	4	5

APPENDIX 2

Assessing Your Overall Fun Work Environment Level

Below are several statements regarding possible occurrences at work. On the scales, indicate the frequency with which you experience the feeling or the activity.

Very Infrequently   **Very Frequently**

1	2	3	4	5

1. I find something to laugh about at work.

1	2	3	4	5

2. I feel happy when I am at work.

1	2	3	4	5

3. I feel that my supervisor is a fun person to work for.

1	2	3	4	5

4. My boss smiles a lot.

1	2	3	4	5

5. I feel that this place is too much fun to leave.

1	2	3	4	5

6. I feel it is fun to work here.

1	2	3	4	5

7. I smile when I tell people about what it's like to work here.

1	2	3	4	5

8. This place lifts my spirits even if I come to work feeling sad.

1	2	3	4	5

9. There are parties and celebrations around here.

1	2	3	4	5

10. My manager takes actions to make this a fun place to be.

1	2	3	4	5

11. I look forward to coming to work.
1   2   3   4   5

12. I hear that people at other organizations don't have the same fun we do working here.
1   2   3   4   5

13. I believe this is an uplifting place to be.
1   2   3   4   5

14. Our customers tell us they think we are one happy group of people.
1   2   3   4   5

15. It makes me feel good to work in this organization.
1   2   3   4   5

16. Humor is used appropriately in this organization.
1   2   3   4   5

17. I enjoy having lunch and breaks with my co-workers.
1   2   3   4   5

18. I joke around with my co-workers.
1   2   3   4   5

19. I socialize with my co-workers after work.
1   2   3   4   5

20. We use humor to lighten up difficult or tense situations.
1   2   3   4   5

Overall total score _____

APPENDIX 3

Perceived Impact of Fun on Organizational Outcomes

Introduction: A fun workplace culture is one in which a variety of formal and informal activities regularly occur that are designed to positively and publicly remind people of their value to their managers, the organization, and each other through the use of humor, playfulness, joyful expressions, opportunities for self satisfaction, or personal recognition.

Directions: Assess your own workplace on the following 10 dimensions, using the five-point response scale as shown. Circle one number for each of the 10 items.

Strongly Disagree   **Strongly Agree**
1   2   3   4   5

1. Having fun at work positively affects employee attitudes (e.g., satisfaction, trust, and enthusiasm).
1   2   3   4   5

2. Having fun at work helps alleviate stress and tension.
1   2   3   4   5

3. Having fun at work results in a higher level of productivity.
1   2   3   4   5

4. Having fun at work results in higher levels of respect and caring for each other.
1   2   3   4   5

5. Having fun at work improves employee work outcomes (e.g., increases employee retention, reduces absenteeism, and increases attendance).
1   2   3   4   5

6. Having fun at work increases employee commitment.
1   2   3   4   5

7. Having fun at work strengthens our corporate culture.
1   2   3   4   5

8. Having fun at work strengthens communications.
1   2   3   4   5

9. Having fun at work positively impacts employee work behaviors (e.g., civility, cooperation, citizenship, fewer complaints of boredom, customer service).
1   2   3   4   5

10. Having fun at work leads to higher quality work.
1   2   3   4   5

Scoring: Add up your scores to the responses for items 1-10. Place your total score here: _____

APPENDIX 4

100 Illustrations of Specific Fun-at-Work Activities*

Baby and wedding showers
Bagel Fridays
Barbeque dinners
Beer-and-banter parties
Birthday cards
Birthday parties
Book fairs
Bowling teams
Brown-bag lunches
Bus trips
Candy-grams
Cartoon-caption contests
Car washes done by executives
Carnival day
Casual dress days
Chili cook-offs
Company picnics
Crazy postcards
Crossword puzzles tailored to the
  organization
Cubicle decorating
Decorated cake contests
Dinner cruises
Dress-alike days
"Dress up your boss" day
Easter bunny visits
Employee-designed T-shirts
"Ethnic food specialties" luncheons
Fake awards/trophies/certificates
Fake letters (outrageous)
Finger painting contest
Foosball table
Free pizza and sodas

Friendly kidnappings
Fun e-mail construction
Funny gift exchange (white elephant)
Gatorade breaks on hot days
Golf tournaments
Guess-the-baby photo contests
Half-day Fridays
Health fairs
Holiday cookie exchanges
Hula hoop contests
Humorous birthday cards
Ice cream socials
Indoor putting contests
Joke exchange day
Jollytologist of the week designate
Juggling scarves
Kazoo day
Latte cart
Limo lottery for a ride to work
Magic tricks
Marble games
Mariachi band
Monthly hikes during lunch
Moving parties
Office decorations
Office Olympics
Office pet days
Office skits
On-site masseuse
On-site theme parks
Orienteering contests
Paintball tournaments
Pajama party breakfasts

Parking lot picnic (tailgate party)
Personal trivia day
Poker walks
Practical jokes
Professional caricature artists
Pumpkin-carving contests
Raffles
Rally races
Relay races
Safety bingo
Scavenger hunts
Shopping sprees
Sing-alongs
Singing telegrams
Softball tournaments
St. Patrick's Day theme decorations
Stress-relief week
Stuffed-animal day

Summer fitness programs
"Thanksgiving leftovers" luncheons
Toasts (sparkling apple juice) to
    successes
Town hall meetings
"Traveling bouquet" of flowers
Turkey shoots
"Ugliest tie" day
Valentine's Day cards
Vanity license plate creation contests
Vending machine give-away days
Video games
Visits by costumed characters
Water gun fights (outdoors)
Welcome Wagon gifts for new hires
Wellness teams
Whitewater raft trips
"Wuzzle-creation" contests

*Adapted from "SHRM Fun Work Environment Survey," Alexandria, VA: SHRM Research, 2002.

APPENDIX 5

A Sampling of Acknowledged Fun Workplaces

AES
AppRiver
Aqualand
Athenahealth
Atlassian
Ben and Jerry's
Beryl Companies
Blazer Industries
CCFC Advertising
CGL
Cold Stone Creamery
Cxtec
Disney
Door to Door Organics
Ernst & Young
GE
Google

Interface Software
Menlo Innovations
Microsoft
Mindlab
NETexponent
New Deal Studios
New Media Strategies
Nike
PeopleSoft
Phoenix Solutions
Pitney Bowes
Pixar
Red Bull London
Root Learning
Southwest Airlines
Time Warner
VW Phaeton Plant

APPENDIX 6

Fun & Humor Websites

http://www.humoru.com

http://positivesharing.com/2007/05/monday-tip-workplace-fun-and-games

http://smallbusinessreview.com/human_resources/Building_a_fun_work_culture

http://www.funatwork.co.uk/

http://www.almorale.com/fun.html

http://www.fisher-price.com/us/hr/fun.asp

http://www.businesstown.com/people/motivation-fun.asp

http://www.fastcompany.com/resources/talent/bksje/100305

http://www.employerhelp.org/jimcollison/stories/naysayer

http://www.deepfun.com

http://www.itstime.com/dec2004.htm

http://home.teleport.com/~laff9to5/injest.html

Join **The Fun Minute Manager** *website!*
Go to **www.TheFunMinuteManager.com**, and register for your free membership.

APPENDIX 7
A Selected Bibliography of Books on Workplace Fun

Bakke, Dennis. *Joy at Work: A CEO's Revolutionary Approach to Fun on the Job.* Seattle: PVG, 2005.

Baylor, Byrd. *I'm in Charge of Celebrations.* New York: Aladdin, 1986.

Blumenfeld, Esther and Lynne Alpern. *Humor at Work: The Guaranteed, Bottom-Line, Low-Cost, High-Efficiency Guide to Success through Humor.* Atlanta: Peachtree, 1994.

Bolman, Lee G. and Terrence E. Deal. *Escape from Cluelessness.* New York: AMACOM, 2000. See especially 111 on "Fun."

Chapman, A.J. and H. C. Foot, eds. *Humor and Laughter: Theory, Research, and Applications.* Hoboken, NJ: Wiley, 1976.

Cousins, Norman. *Anatomy of an Illness.* Toronto: Bantam Books, 1981.

Crother, Cyndi. *Catch! A Fishmonger's Guide to Greatness.* San Francisco: Berrett-Koehler, 2005.

Deal, Terrence E. and M. K. Key. *Corporate Celebration: Play, Purpose, and Profit at Work.* San Francisco: Berrett-Koehler, 1998. See especially 107-115, "Play at work: Fun ignites energy," and 205-212, "Recapturing joy at work."

DeForest, C. "The Art of Celebration." In *Transforming Leadership: From Vision to Results,* edited by J.D. Adams, 223. Alexandria, VA: Miles River Press, 1986.

Fahlman, Clyde. *Laughing Nine to Five: The Quest for Humor in the Workplace.* Portland, OR: Steelhead Press, 1997.

Firth, David. *How to Make Work Fun: An Alphabet of Possibilities.* Aldershot, UK: Gower, 1995.

Firth, David and Alan Leigh. *The Corporate Fool.* Hoboken, NJ: Wiley, 2001.

Glanz, Barbara. *Care Packages: Dozens of Little Things You Can Do to Regenerate Spirit at Work.* New York: McGraw-Hill, 1996.

Goldblatt, Joe. *Special Events: The Art and Science of Celebration.* New York: Van Nostrand Reinhold, 1990.

Goodman, Joel. *Laffirmations: 1001 Ways to Add Humor to Your Life and Work.* Deerfield Beach, FL: Health Communications Inc, 1995.

Greenwich, Carolyn. *Fun and Gains.* New York: McGraw-Hill, 2001.—. *The Fun Factor.* New York: McGraw-Hill, 1997.

Hemsath, Dave and Leslie Yerkes. *301 More Ways to Have Fun at Work.* San Francisco: Berrett-Koehler, 2001.

—. *301 Ways to Have Fun at Work.* San Francisco: Berrett-Koehler, 1997. See especially 184-212, "Simple acts of fun," and 216-229, "A twelve-step method to fun."

Iapoce, M. *A Funny Thing Happened on the Way to the Boardroom: Using Humor in Business Speaking.* Hoboken, NJ: Wiley, 1988.

Kouzes, James M. and Barry Z. Posner. *Encouraging the Heart.* San Francisco: Jossey-Bass, 1999. See especially 113-127, "Celebrate Together," and 136 and 142.

Leider, Richard J., et al. *Whistle While You Work*. San Francisco: Berrett-Koehler, 2001.

Lundin, Stephen C., Harry Paul, and John Christensen. *Fish!* New York: Hyperion, 2000. See especially 62-66 on "Play."

Morreall, John. *Humor Works: The Benefits of Humor in the Workplace*. Amherst, MA: HRD Press, 1997.

Nelson, Bob. *1001 Ways to Energize Employees*. New York: Workman Publishing, 1997.

Newman, Winifred Barnum. *Gumwrappers and Goggles*. San Antonio, TX: Summit Publishing Co., 1982.

Newstrom, John, and Edward Scannell. *The Big Book of Presentation Games: Wake-Em-Up Tricks, Ice Breakers, & Other Fun Stuff*. New York: McGraw-Hill, 1998.

Paulson, Terry. *Making Humor Work: Take Your Job Seriously and Yourself Lightly*. Mississauga, ON: Crisp Learning, 1989.

Putzier, John. *Get Weird: 101 Innovative Ways to Make Your Company a Great Place to Work*. New York: AMACOM, 2001.

Richards, Dick. *Artful Work: Awakening Joy, Meaning, and Commitment in the Workplace*. San Francisco: Berrett-Koehler, 1995.

Sanitate, Frank. *Don't Go To Work Unless It's Fun*. Santa Barbara, CA: Santa Barbara Press, 1994.

Scannell, E.E. and John W. Newstrom. *Games Trainers Play*. New York: McGraw-Hill, 1980.

Sikorski, Joy. *How to Draw a Radish: And Other Fun Things to Do at Work*. San Francisco: Chronicle, 1995.

Stearns, F.R. *Laughing: Physiology, Pathophysiology, Psychology, Pathopsychology, and Development*. Springfield, IL: Charles Thomas, 1972.

Weinstein, Matt and Joel Goodman. *Playfair: Everybody's Guide to Noncompetitive Play*. San Luis Obispo, CA: Impact Publishers, 1980.

Weinstein, Matt. *Managing to Have Fun*. New York: Fireside Books, 1996.

Weinstein, Matt and Luke Barber. *Work Like Your Dog*. New York: Villard Books, 1999.

West, Edie. *201 Icebreakers: Group Mixers, Warm-Ups, Energizers, and Playful Activities*. New York: McGraw-Hill, 1997.

Wilson, Larrry, and Hersch Wilson. *Play to Win!: Choosing Growth over Fear in Work and Life*. Austin, TX: Bard Press, 1998.

Yerkes, Leslie. *Fun Works: Creating Places Where People Like To Work*. San Francisco: Berrett-Koehler, 2001.

Yokohama, John and John Michelli. *When Fish Fly: Lessons for Creating a Vital and Energized Workplace Like the World Famous Pike Place Fish Market*. New York: Hyperion, 2004.

Seminars from The Bob Pike Group

Bob Pike's Creative Training Techniques™ Boot Camp
Updated for 2009, this two-day workshop will show you how to transform your training into a more participant-centered learning experience and is publicly presented over one hundred times each year in the United States.

Bob Pike's Creative Training Techniques™ Boot Camp Plus
This is the basic Boot Camp material with a third day added for application. Bring one of your own projects with so you can CTT-ize it! You will get immediate feedback from peers and a Bob Pike Group training consultant.

Presentation Skills for Trainers and Subject Matter Experts
Improve your presentation skills! This workshop focuses on the basics of adult learning, body language and delivery style with many chances to practice in a safe environment. Use this knowledge to communicate more effectively, with better results.

Instructional Design for Participant-Centered Learning
Dig deeper into the principles of participant-centered training methods and apply them to current material. This workshop is for instructional designers, instructional design managers and training managers who want to design more effective training.

Getting Started with e-Learning
To help you avoid costly e-learning mistakes, The Bob Pike Group partnered with William Horton Consulting to develop this workshop on the fundamentals of e-learning. This content-rich, highly interactive workshop lets you examine the essential e-learning terminology, tools, technology, and best practices.

Webinars with a WOW Factor
It's time to put WOW back into your webinar! Design creative webinars and increase retention and ultimately the transfer of learning, including what to do before and after the webinar, to get the most out of the session.

Bonus Resources
Go to our website to download a free copy of Bob's e-book *Unlock the Power to Learn* and a timer he uses in his workshops. www.BobPikeGroup.com/pages.asp?pageid=33777

To sign up for The Bob Pike Group's free monthly ezine, which is filled with creative tips and discussions on best practices, go to www.BobPikeGroup.com/pages.asp?pageid=37783

Bob Pike's Training and Performance Improvement Conference

Your company is now facing new threats, new competitors and new challenges like never before. Performance is all that counts. Training directors and corporate trainers need new tools and new technologies to produce the measurable results that management is now demanding to transform your organization! Are you ready?

The Bob Pike Group designed this event to challenge everything you know about training and to transform that knowledge into useful, powerful techniques and skill sets for you to use.

Bob Pike's Training and Performance Improvement Conference is the only conference dedicated exclusively to the participant-centered approach to training

- Learn about the revolutionary, participant-centered training approach—the breakthrough alternative to lecture-based training
- See the nation's leading training consultants model their very best participant-centered activities
- Experience the power of participant-centered techniques to dramatically increase retention
- Learn about innovative training transfer techniques adopted by leading Fortune 500 companies
- Discover powerful management strategies that clearly demonstrate the business results for your training programs

For information on any of these public workshops or in-house offerings , call The Bob Pike Group at (800) 383-9210 or go to www.BobPikeGroup.com.

More Great Resources from Creative Training Techniques!

SCORE! TWO

By Rich Meiss and Bob Pike

Participants in a typical training only retain about 20 percent of the information within 21 days of training. Activities in this book are designed to have learners strategically interacting with your material to increase their retention to 80 percent or more! This book holds 70 closers, openers, review methods and energizers you can immediately use. **$40**

POWERFUL PRESENTATIONS, VOLUME 2

By Bob Pike and Betsy Allen

Create a powerful presentation in five minutes or less! Designing training that sticks doesn't have to take hours. Use these 52 graphic organizers, audience-centered learning activities, and bounce-back strategies to create a total-body learning experience that helps anchor key concepts of your training. **$24.95**

ONE-ON-ONE

By Bob Pike, Lynn Solem and Dave Arch

One-on-One Training gives you both the theory and practice behind this powerful method. You'll learn about the basic tenets of adult learning, and you'll get practical tips on keeping training participants focused. Plus, you'll get an array of training activities specially designed for one-on-one training.

Fast, inexpensive and effective, one-on-one training could be right for you. Put this practical primer to work today! $34.95

To order these titles, call Creative Training Techniques Press at 866-368-5653 or go to our website at www.CreativeTrainingTech.com.

REVITALIZE YOUR TRAINING INSTANTLY

With a subscription to Bob Pike's Creative Training Techniques newsletter.

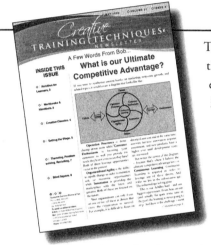

This monthly publication offers more quick tips, openers, closers and activities for engaging your participants and helping increase retention. Immediately applicable and adaptable to your training, these techniques will give you a head start on making your training participant-centered. In addition, the Creative Training Techniques newsletter website also has a searchable archive with hundreds of additional activities, tips and techniques by Bob Pike or submitted by readers since the newsletter's inception in 1988. A can't-miss resource! Silver-level subscription includes a hard copy and digital access to each monthly newsletter, and twice-monthly article updates. Gold-level subscription includes a hard copy, digital access, twice-monthly article updates, access to audio and video versions of techniques, and a member's-only forum.

TO ORDER

Go to www.CreativeTrainingTech.com
or call 866-368-5653
(1-612-454-2542 for international).

JOIN US!

Many of the ideas for adding fun and productivity to the workplace came from the many clients we've worked with over the years. Here's your chance to share your ideas and get published. Send any ideas you've actually used in the workplace using the format below to CTTEditor@CreativeTrainingTech.com. Your idea may appear in a future issue of Creative Training Techniques newsletter as well as future editions of *The Fun Minute Manager.*

Here's my idea: _____

Here's how it worked: _____

Here's what you need to be careful of: _____

Here's the result: _____

Name_____

Title _____

Organization_____

Street Address, City, State, Zip Code, Country_____

Phone Number_____

Email Address_____